# WRITING EFFECTIVE NEWS RELEASES...

## HOW TO GET FREE PUBLICITY FOR YOURSELF, YOUR BUSINESS, OR YOUR ORGANIZATION

CATHERINE V. MCINTYRE

PICCADILLY BOOKS
COLORADO SPRINGS. COLORADO

Cover design by Robin Axtell

Copyright © 2005, 1992, Catherine V. McIntyre

All rights reserved.  No part of this book may be reproduced in any form or by any electronic or mechanical means without permission in writing from the publisher, except by a reviewer who may quote brief passages in a review.

**Piccadilly Books**
P.O. Box 25203
Colorado Springs, CO 80936
www.piccadillybooks.com


**Library of Congress Cataloging-in-Publication Data**

McIntyre, Catherine V.
    Writing effective news releases: how to get free publicity for yourself, your business, or your organization /
Catherine V. McIntyre.
          p.        cm.
    Includes bibliographical references and index.
    ISBN 0-941599-19-1
    1. Publicity.  2. Public relations.  3. Press releases--Authorship.  I. Title.
HD59.M35  1992
659.2--dc20                                        91-45516


Printed in Canada

# DEDICATION AND ACKNOWLEDGMENTS

I dedicate this book to my friend and former editor, Irene O'Sullivan, without whose encouragement and helpful suggestions this book could not have been written.

I wish to express my thanks to all the editors of newspapers and the television and radio producers around the country who took time from their busy schedules to make contributions to this book, and to the family entertainers, business persons, publishers, authors, publicity chairpersons, and publicity/public relations experts who contributed news releases.

My special thanks to the librarians at the El Cajon, California, Public Library for their cheerful and knowledgeable help with my research. I am convinced they are all geniuses.

Credit is given to the following for permission to reprint material used in this book. Sally Hazzard, San Diego County Department of Animal Control; Judy Cullins, Skills Unlimited; Dorothy Johnson, Martin Luther King Jr. Federal Holiday Planning Comittee; Dave Alexander, Radio Station KKHT-FM; *Daily American Republic*; Jan Eastman; Paul Barton; *Uptown*; *San Diego Metropolitan*; Jean Ross Peterson; Simon & Schuster; Avon Books; Jennifer Nestegard, Queen Mary and Spruce Goose; *Business Tokyo*; R.J. Garis, Publicity International Agency; *The Daily Californian*; Stuart Robertshaw; Barbara Brabec; Niki Scott; Silvana Clark, Memory Makers; Chris Anderson, Mountain Empire School; *The Alpine Sun*; John Turner, Ghost Communications; *San Diego Family Press*; Loch David Crane; *Ramona Sentinel*; *San Diego Reader*; HarperCollins Publishers; Elaine M. Brooks, Lisa Ekus Public Relations Company; Cate Terwilliger, *Colorado Springs Gazette Telegraph*; Vicki Lansky; Eldonna P. Lay; *The Southtown Economist*; Marin Small Publishers Association; Karen Misuraca, Lagoon Publications; Barbara Brown, United Service Organizations; *The Southwest Times Record*; Donna Guttman, Mercy Hospital and Medical Center.

# TABLE OF CONTENTS

# FOREWORD

News releases addressed to editors who are dead or retired still arrive at the newspaper where I have worked for more than 26 years. Some are from distant places and publicize events and products in which this newspaper, whose coverage is primarily local, has little or no interest. These are the news releases that clutter desks for a few days and eventually find their way to the wastebasket.

The Associated Press recently dispatched a story about a survey that revealed how press releases sent to Southern California newsrooms are handled. The study showed the newsrooms receive an average of 122 news releases each day. One reported it received up to 600 a day. Editors participating in the survey said less than 20 percent were useful.

This says something about the need to properly target the audience you are trying to reach and to occasionally update mailing lists. It should not be interpreted as blanket condemnation of the news release or its value when appropriately written and sent to the right publications.

My experience has been that reporters and editors rely on news releases more than they like to admit. They cannot be everywhere and know everything that is going on. News releases frequently are the launching pads for good stories.

In this book, Catherine McIntyre describes how to write effective news releases by focusing on the news values that are required for any well-written story. These values are not difficult to understand, but they are often neglected, especially by the novice writer of news releases. She also has included valuable tips on dealing with newspapers and the electronic media to assure the best results from your efforts.

Those wishing to publicize business ventures, their own books, or entertaining performances will find specific advice in Chapters 6, 7, and 8. Publicists for clubs, lodges, churches and other non-profit organizations—individuals who tend to be appointed for this job more often because they are faithful members than for their writing skills—will find Chapter 9 especially helpful.

Writing effective news releases, directed to the right audiences, will accomplish your purpose and the purpose of the publication whose help you solicit. Good releases will generate more publicity for your organization, and from the newspaper's point of view, will transmit valuable information to readers, informing, educating or amusing them.

When this occurs, everybody wins.

Del Hood
Associate Editor, *The Daily Californian*

# CHAPTER 1

# THE VALUE OF FREE PUBLICITY

Would you like to double your profits? To have your name or the name of your business instantly recognized by all who hear it? Or run for public office without spending much money? Or raise thousands of dollars for your favorite charity?

If so, you need PUBLICITY!

All these benefits...and more...can be yours as soon as the local and/or national press, television, and radio stations start giving publicity to you, your business, or your organization.

Yes, that can happen to you!

Judy Cullins, director of Skills Unlimited of La Mesa, California, received more than 300 calls within two days after information on her memory improvement seminars appeared in a local newspaper column. She filled two seminars, rather than the one originally planned, and received bookings from other organizations for two additional six-hour seminars at $1,000 each.

Scott Innes, a disc jockey in Springfield, Missouri, gained regional fame for the record he and his son made, entitled "Dear Daddy: The Wind Beneath My Wings." After newspapers ran his story and radio stations aired his recording, record sales increased by twenty percent.

"Dr. Humor," known in real life as Dr. Stuart Robertshaw is a professor of psychology at the University of Wisconsin. He was able to further his research on humor after newspapers and magazines carried articles about his organization, called the National Association for the Humor Impaired. Within eight months of his first effort at getting publicity, Dr. Humor had been a guest on ninety-seven radio talk shows and had been approached about appearing on the Phil Donahue, the Oprah Winfrey, and the David Letterman television shows. Within a year of the first news coverage, his organization had gained more than 900 members and was still growing. Called "honcho of hee-haws" by *Family Circle*, Dr. Robertshaw has gone on to gain great popularity on the national speakers circuit.

Although the backgrounds and aims of these people were diverse, the way the publicity was generated was the same in each case. None of these people were professional publicists, nor did they use the services of publicists. None had to resort to elaborate publicity campaigns, complete with press kits and photographs.

All of them got publicity through one simple method: Writing an effective news release.

And you can do it, too.

Regardless of what you want to promote, you need to get the public's attention in order to be successful. Whether you are trying to sell cars or cosmetics on the national level, or cakes and quilts at the local church bazaar, your potential customers have to know your products or services are available if you want to succeed.

There are two ways to get the public's attention: Advertising and publicity.

What's the difference between the two?

Several thousands of dollars per page!

You must *pay* for advertising, but publicity is virtually "free."

Large corporations spend millions on advertising each year. They routinely pay $30,000 to $50,000 *or more* for full page ads in national magazines to draw attention to and promote their products. A half-page advertisement in a newspaper with a circulation of around 100,000 runs about $2,000 per day. And, since rates are based on how many people the advertisement will reach, even a *small* display ad in a newspaper with a very large circulation (1,000,000 or more), runs as much as $3,000...FOR ONE DAY!

If you don't have that kind of money to toss around to promote your product, service, or organization, then your alternative is to generate free publicity.

That's where news releases come in.

A news release, often called a *press release*, is a written announcement about an interesting aspect of a person, business, service, or organization. The release is sent to newspapers, magazines, or radio and television stations for the purpose of informing the media and, in turn, is used by the media to inform the public.

News releases can generate huge amounts of publicity.

Big companies know this. In addition to buying advertising, they pay large salaries to employees in their publicity/public relations departments or hire professional publicists to write and send out news releases. They constantly use news releases to announce new product lines, new branch openings, and personnel changes.

Regardless of the type of business being promoted, whether it is a record company, a real estate firm, or a restaurant chain, these news releases generate volumes of publicity and keep the companies' names or the names of their products before the public.

Would big companies bother sending news releases if this method of getting publicity did not help increase business and/or profits? Not on your life! News releases work for them.

And if news releases work for big companies, they can also work for you. Whether you want to promote seminars, songs, or soap powder, a good news release can generate publicity. Since it costs you nothing but paper and postage, a news release is the cheapest, most effective way to get publicity, whether you are a comedian or corporate executive, master craftsman, or magician.

You might ask, "But if that's the case, why doesn't everyone do it?"

Many do.

Newspapers, magazines, television and radio stations receive hundreds and hundreds of news releases every month. The majority, however, are tossed in the trash.

Why?

Because they are not effective.

They have no "zing." They do not include news values. They do not contain complete information. And, to put it bluntly, they are simply not newsworthy.

According to Lizanne Poppins, editor of the home and garden section of the *San Diego Union*, San Diego, California, "About eighty percent of the news releases we get are thrown in the trash immediately. They are either poorly written and don't contain complete information or they are inappropriate. We receive many from all over the nation that just do not apply to our area. It's obvious they have not studied our format before submitting. A news release has got to be of interest to our readers before it gets our attention."

Editor Jack Moseley, *Southwest Times Record*, Fort Smith, Arkansas, also cites lack of regional interest as a reason for trashing a news release.

"Some of the news releases we receive have nothing to do with our area," Moseley says. "I don't know why people even waste their postage. With the volume of mail we receive, it's annoying to have to wade through so much garbage to find the pearls. It's also annoying when the most important aspect of a potential story is buried at the bottom of a news release instead of at the top where it belongs. I'm sure a lot of good stories have been missed by a lot of newspapers because the information wasn't presented properly."

These complaints are common to editors all over the country. So, if you don't want *your* news release to be among the eighty percent tossed in the "circular file," read on.

Whatever you need to promote, whether it is your business in order to increase profits, or your service club's next fund-raiser, this book will show you how to write effective news releases that will get media attention.

Even if you have never considered yourself a good writer, you will come to understand, through instruction and actual examples, just how to construct your news release and what information it should contain. You will learn how to include news values that will make your news releases so newsworthy an editor or producer will *want* to give you coverage.

In other words, you will learn how to get what you really want...SUCCESS by generating free publicity.

## NEWS RELEASES VERSUS ADVERTISING

The major advantages of using news releases as opposed to advertising are the lower cost and higher response. Advertising can cost thousands of dollars and may or may not be effective. News releases cost only a fraction of the amount and usually produce better results. It has been estimated that editorial coverage is generally about seven times as effective as paid advertising.

In one example, a computer software company paid $6,000 to advertise a new software program in a national computer magazine. The company received 100 responses to this ad. In another similar computer magazine the same software program was given a free favorable editorial review. This review resulted in nearly 900 inquiries. The editorial out-pulled the paid advertisement 9 to 1.

This ratio of response is to be expected because people trust editorials as unbiased opinions. People are naturally skeptical of any claims in an ad because they know the company is trying to sell something. Editorials, on the other hand, are trying to relay useful information to readers.

The major advantage of paid advertising is that you can control the content of the ad and the time and place it is published. In many instances paid advertising is necessary.

All businesses can benefit by seeking free publicity through news releases. For some small businesses with limited budgets, this is the only way they can effectively publicize themselves.

# CHAPTER 2

# WHAT IS A NEWS RELEASE?

The fact that eighty percent of the news releases received by the media are tossed in the wastebasket might discourage some people.

But before you let yourself be intimidated by that fact, consider this: All branches of the media NEED good news releases. They depend on receiving them, *for a large part of the news is generated by news releases.*

News comes from a variety of sources:

1) Original reporting (meaning that a reporter either covers a certain beat to gather information or gets an idea himself/herself, with no prompting from an outside source, and digs out the information)
2) Wire services
3) Word-of-mouth and/or telephone tips
4) News releases

Of these sources, only twenty-five to fifty percent of the news, generally speaking, comes from wire services or original reporting. *The rest is generated by tips and news releases.*

These figures will vary from publication to publication and from one branch of the media to another, but they give you an idea of why news releases are needed by the media.

The reason so many news releases are not used is that many people who send out news releases do not know how to make a news release newsworthy and, because they are untrained, they fail to give the newspapers or other media what they need. But, by reading this book, you will have an edge over the competition and should have no problem getting publicity.

If you're a novice at writing news releases, it's possible that you do not know what a news release looks like, much less what should go into one. Don't worry. I have examples.

Although formats vary, the following is a general outline of how a news release is set up.

Now that you have a map, let's discuss the landmarks.

RELEASE INFORMATION LINE                    Name of Contact Person

                                            Telephone Number of Contact

Date


The Subject


ATTENTION-GRABBING HEADLINE


The body of the news release begins here. In this section, give all the pertinent facts you wish

to convey. Avoid flowery language in giving the information.


Type double spaced. Block style is preferable with extra spaces between paragraphs.


Leave wide margins (about 1-$\frac{1}{2}$ to 2") because editors need the space to make notes on the

copy. If using a computer, DO NOT justify the right margin.


Make sure your grammar, spelling, and punctuation are correct, for errors mark you as a

careless amateur and turn off editors.


Keep your paragraphs short and punchy.


INDICATION OF "END" OR "MORE"

*Basic news release format.*

## WHAT A NEWS RELEASE SHOULD CONTAIN

Although announcements in various forms sometimes pass for news releases, there are certain characteristics all good news releases have in common. The following is a discussion of each aspect.

### Identifying the Sending Entity

A good news release shows at a glance who sent it. Some of the best news releases are on letterhead paper with the name, address, and telephone number of the person, business, or organization clearly shown at the top. However, if letterhead paper is not available, it is acceptable to type in this information at the top of the sheet.

Some references advise against using letterhead and suggest plain white paper or special news release paper. However, special news release stationery is expensive and unnecessary unless you will be sending out hundreds of news releases.

If everyone sent news releases on plain white paper with no identification at the top editors would soon be tearing their hair and screaming. For, at a glance, all the news releases would look alike. Trying to relocate one particular news release within the stacks on his/her desk would be a nightmare. Each one would have to be reread to identify it. It would be like putting together a jigsaw puzzle of all white pieces...very time consuming.

Letterhead or a typed heading identifies you or your organization immediately and distinguishes your news release from the others in the stack. When you start sending consistently good news releases, that familiar letterhead or typed heading will get the editor's prompt attention and will be welcomed.

### News Release Information Line

A couple of spaces below the letterhead, you should type, in CAPITAL LETTERS, one of the following release information lines:

FOR IMMEDIATE RELEASE
FOR RELEASE ON: (Date)
RELEASE AT WILL
COMMUNITY CALENDAR LISTING
PUBLIC SERVICE ANNOUNCEMENT

These release information lines tell the media: (1) that this is a news release, and (2) when it is appropriate to use the material.

Since many people seem to be confused by when to use which release information line, the following is a brief discussion of each one.

FOR IMMEDIATE RELEASE

If time is a factor, use this release information line. A couple of spaces below the line, list the date you sent it. (Without a sending date, how is the media to know when is "immediate"?)

A lot of people slap this line on all their releases, yet do not bother to list a date when it was sent. This can end up having an adverse effect because, unlike many businesses, newspaper personnel do not usually date-stamp incoming mail. There is no need, because the pieces of paper will not be hanging around an editor's desk for very long. With the volume of mail the average newspaper receives every day, the information will be used or tossed within a very short time.

Editors often receive news releases marked "FOR IMMEDIATE RELEASE" that quite obviously are *not* time-sensitive. If such a release looks interesting, but there is no room in the next couple of editions, an editor may stick it in a drawer or a pending file for use in a later issue. When it next surfaces, the editor may not remember if it is a week old or a month old, if no sending date is listed. Rather than publish material that may be outdated, the editor will probably just toss it.

The situation just described may make it seem that editors are not well organized. Certainly there are some who are very well organized. The problem is that hundreds of news releases cross their desks every week. The sheer volume of information with which they deal is enough to boggle anyone's mind.

So, for the reasons listed above, if your news release is time-sensitive, do put "FOR IMMEDIATE RELEASE," but list a sending date.

FOR RELEASE ON: (Date)

This release information line is used when you are sending a news release in advance of the time you want the information publicized.

For example, if you are opening a new branch of your business in a distant city and you will be in that city for the opening, you would want the media in that city to know in advance that you are coming.

Why?

Because a reporter might want to contact you to arrange an interview while you are there and do a feature story on you and your business.

At the same time, you would not want the information about your big opening to be publicized too far in advance of the event.

Say your new branch is opening on November 12, 2005. If the city is large, its daily newspaper(s) will have a business section in every day's edition. In that case you might want to use "FOR RELEASE ON: November 10, 2005." That would get the information to the public two days in advance of the opening.

However, many mid-sized newspapers include a business section only once or twice a week. Therefore, they might not be able to print the information on the day you state. If the business section comes out only on Friday, and you have indicated that you want the information released on November 10, then the first date the information could be published after the designated date would be on November 13, the day *after* your opening. If you are hoping to draw the public, that would do you no good.

So, it's better to give at least a week's leeway between the date the information can be released and the event.

Another example of when delaying publicity is desirable is when publicizing a book. It could be that you do not want information released about the book until copies are available in local stores. Since these news releases go out in volume and must be prepared far in advance, it is appropriate to use "FOR RELEASE AFTER: (date)." By that date, the books would be in the stores.

But that line would not be wise on your business opening, for if you stated, "FOR RELEASE AFTER: November 6, 2005," editors may assume that it would be all right to use the information on November 13.

In the case of your business opening, a better release information line would be "FOR RELEASE BETWEEN: November 6 and November 10, 2005."

That would tell the media exactly when it would be appropriate to print the information.

The release information line showing a requested date of release is especially appropriate when you want to give the media plenty of advance notice, yet do not want the information to be released to the public until a later date.

RELEASE AT WILL

This release information line is appropriate when time is not a factor.

For example, say you make "widgets" and you want the public to know. But you've been making widgets for years and you plan to continue making widgets until you die. It does not matter when your news release is used, as long as the media uses it sometime.

If the information you are supplying is timeless, it is not necessary to date the news release.

## COMMUNITY CALENDAR LISTING

This release information line is appropriate when you are announcing an upcoming event for a non-profit organization.

Most newspapers have a section in which charitable events, such as fund-raising fashion shows, award dinners, or club installation luncheons are listed. The blurbs are usually only one or two paragraphs long, but they alert the public and can increase attendance at the functions.

## PUBLIC SERVICE ANNOUNCEMENTS

This release information line is for the same purpose as the Community Calendar Listing above, but is used when sending an announcement to the electronic media.

PSA's, as they are called, are very brief spot announcements that stations carry as a service to the community. They are explained more fully in Chapter 5.

A release information line is usually, but not always, shown in the upper left-hand corner of the sheet a couple of lines down from the letterhead. Many news releases include the words "NEWS RELEASE" or "PRESS RELEASE" near the top of the page; however, as soon as an editor sees the words "FOR IMMEDIATE RELEASE," etc., the editor knows it is a news release.

### The Contact Person

The name and telephone number of the contact person should appear on the opposite side of the page from the release information line.

Above all, a news release must have the NAME AND TELEPHONE NUMBER OF THE CONTACT PERSON. This cannot be emphasized too strongly.

Often media personnel have questions after they read a news release. You may think you have included every bit of information the media could possibly need or want, but you would be amazed at how often essential information is omitted.

One TV reporter friend tells about the time he got a news release on a seemingly news-worthy event. He was all set to round up a camera crew and go cover it. But there was no address listed and no telephone number for a contact person. Sending the release was just a waste of postage.

Even if the address had been listed, the reporter may have wanted to call to find out what the cross streets were and the easiest route to take to get there.

Many times a news release will prompt enough interest that a reporter will want to do a feature story on you and/or your business or organization. This is the type of publicity business owners dream of. But a reporter would need the name and telephone number of a contact person in order to gather additional information and perhaps get a quote or two. If that information is not listed, you lose out on a great opportunity for free publicity.

Trust me on this one. Editors and reporters can think up more questions than most people have answers for. So be sure you list the name and telephone number of a contact person.

### The Subject

On the left side of the page, a couple of spaces below the name and telephone number of the contact person, some news releases—although not all—list the subject. The subject, if listed, should be underlined.

The subject line should be as short as possible, such as: Installation Luncheon, New Product Line, or Increasing Profits. It should be just enough that an editor or producer will know at a glance what you are writing about.

The electronic media, especially, like to see a subject line.

## Headline

A couple of spaces below the subject (if one is listed), type, in CAPITAL LETTERS, an attention-grabbing headline.

Some older books on working with the press have stated that headlines should not be used on news releases. Statements were made that editors had been known to react violently when someone presumed to tell them what the news value of a story was by writing a headline.

Well, I've seen editors react violently from time to time, but never because a news release had a headline that showed news value. The editors I've been associated with are delighted when a headline summarizes the news values involved in a story.

Of course, you can't expect your headline to be used on the printed article. An editor will write the final headline for the resulting story, and what is written often depends on the space available.

The headline serves as another distinguishing aspect of your news release and helps the editor find it if it has perversely crawled back into the stack with the other news releases on the editor's desk.

The main benefit of a headline, however, is getting the editor's attention and generating interest in what follows.

## The Body

This isn't the kind of body that's buried in a mystery. But sometimes it's a mystery to editors why the most important information is buried in the body of a news release...often way at the bottom.

The body is the main part of your news release, where you tell your story.

It starts three or four lines below the headline and should be double spaced for easier reading by tired, overworked eyes.

The most significant aspect of a story should be at the beginning with additional information given in declining order of importance. The information should cover what journalists call "The Five W's": Who, What, When, Where and Why. (Sometimes it is pertinent to include a sixth—How.) These will be explained more fully later in this chapter.

## End or More

Two spaces below your last line, you should put "-30-" or more commonly "###". Both of these indicate the end, and tell an editor there is not another page roaming around the desk somewhere.

One page news releases are desirable, but if you must use more space, put the word "more" two spaces below the last line of the first page. Also, identify the second page with the subject and page number in case the pages get separated on a busy editor's desk. To be safe, staple the two sheets together in the upper left hand corner.

If your news release does run to two pages, generally the second page goes on a separate sheet rather than on the back of the first sheet.

## NEWS RELEASE EXAMPLES

Although formats vary from news release to news release, the example you are about to see has all the major elements which should be included.

1) It shows who sent it and the originator's address.
2) It shows it is a news release.
3) It shows a release information line.
4) It shows the date the release was sent out.
5) It shows the name and telephone number of the contact person(s).
6) It has an informational headline.
7) The body includes complete information.

Take a moment and examine the release on the following two pages.

# news release

PUBLIC AFFAIRS OFFICE ● COUNTY ADMINISTRATION CENTER
1600 PACIFIC HIGHWAY ● SAN DIEGO, CALIFORNIA 92101-2422

## FOR IMMEDIATE RELEASE

**DATE:**  July 18, 1990                    **CONTACT:** Sally B. Hazzard

Marco A. Anguiano

(619) 531-6041

### PADRES PITCHERS RALLY AT PET BENEFIT LUNCHEON

The sixth annual **Pitchers for Pets** luncheon to benefit abandoned, injured and homeless animals at the County of San Diego Animal Shelters will be held on Sunday, July 29, 1990 from 11:00 a.m. to 12:30 p.m. in the Roof Garden Club at San Diego Jack Murphy Stadium.

This event is open to the public, but reservations are required.  The event is sponsored by the County of San Diego Department of Animal Control with the help of the San Diego Padres baseball team and will benefit various projects that help nurture lost and abandoned pet back to health and to prepare them for adoption. **Pitchers for Pets** also funds public education about the importance of spaying and neutering.

-more-

-2-

The Padre pitchers will be on hand to sign photos for fans at the event. Admission of $25 includes a **Pitchers for Pets** T-shirt and a game ticket for that afternoon's Padres game against the Houston Astros at 1:05 pm. Reservations must be made by July 25.

For more information and reservations call 531-6041.

# # #

As you can see, this news release covered the "Five W's" in the body.

**WHO**: County of San Diego Department of Animal Control and the San Diego Padres baseball team

**WHAT**: 6th Annual Pitchers for Pets luncheon

**WHEN**: 11 a.m. to 12:30 p.m., Sunday, July 29, 1990

**WHERE**: Roof Garden Club at San Diego Jack Murphy Stadium*

**WHY**: To raise money to benefit abandoned, injured, and homeless animals and provide public education about the importance of spaying and neutering

This news release also includes additional useful information, such as the price of the ticket ($25) and what the public will get (in addition to lunch) for that $25: a Pitchers for Pets T-shirt, a ticket for that afternoon's game, and a signed photo from a favorite Padre baseball player.

Now that you understand the format and what kind of information your news release should contain, let's deal with content.

In order to determine what you're going to write, the first question you should ask yourself is, "What am I trying to sell?"

Yes, SELL. Getting publicity is a form of marketing. Even if you are only trying to publicize your church bazaar, you are trying to sell people on the idea of attending.

So determine in your own mind what it is you are selling. Are you selling yourself as a political candidate? Are you selling your hand-crafted items? Are you selling your services as a

family entertainer, such as a clown or magician? Or are you trying to sell tickets to your women's club's fashion show?

Once it is clear what you are selling, ask yourself, "*For the public*, what is the most important thing I'm trying to publicize?"

If you are trying to sell yourself, what is it about you that makes you desirable for the position you seek? Is it your unique background, your years of experience, or your level of expertise that will help you get the job done?

If you are trying to sell a product, what is it about the product that is new, improved, or different in some way? How will the public benefit by using your product? Will it make life more comfortable for them? Will it make their homes look better? Will it drive away pesky bugs and rodents? Will it make a brother-in-law want to go to work?

If it is a service you are offering, what makes your service valuable to the public? Will it straighten out their tax mess? Will it improve their personalities? Will it make them more beautiful?

*Benefit to the public*, i.e., readers, viewers, or listeners, is what will grab an editor's or producer's attention, for they know that their audience wants to know "What's in it for me?"

Let's take an example mentioned earlier.

Judy Cullins, director of Skills Unlimited of La Mesa, California, knows from experience that an effective news release can generate free publicity and improve business. But she also realizes that her services must be of benefit to the public before she can expect to get publicity.

Cullins, who describes herself as a "freelance entrepreneur," conducts seminars on a variety of topics. The news release on page 21 for a seminar on improving one's memory produced dynamic results.

First, she received a telephone call from the newspaper asking for additional information

---

*Ordinarily, the address would be given, but San Diego's Jack Murphy Stadium is so well known, it was not necessary here.

**FOR IMMEDIATE RELEASE**

                              CONTACT: Judy Cullins, Director
                              SKILLS UNLIMITED
                              7000 Melody Lane
                              La Mesa, CA 92042

                              Telephone: 466-0622

Free Memory Improvement Seminar

                    WAKE UP YOUR MIND

Do you have trouble remembering important things, people's names
or where you left your keys?  Do you read a paragraph and then
wonder what it said?  This popular VITAL LIVING SKILLS  seminar
meets on nine Tuesdays from 1 to 4 p.m., from February 5 through
April 9.

Learn about memory myths, why you forget, how memory works and ten
ways to expand your memory instantly.  Experience mind-mapping, a
unique color-coded way to take notes and a five-step reading
strategy to increase concentration, speed and recall.

Sponsored by La Mesa Senior Center, 8450 La Mesa Blvd., La Mesa,
this free seminar is open to all ages.  Texts are available at the
first meeting.  To register, just show up or call instructor, Judy
Cullins, M.A., at 466-0622.

                         ###

and comments. The news release and telephone interview prompted the *San Diego Union* to use the information as its lead item in a popular column.

The public was obviously interested in learning more about the subject, for Cullins received more than 250 calls within 24 hours of the time this small piece appeared and more than 100 calls came in during the following days. After filling the seminar's quota to the absolute maximum (150), she was forced to put a message on her answering machine telling callers that the seminar had been filled, and giving instructions on how they could register for another seminar scheduled for a later date.

And how did this response benefit Cullins, since these seminars were free?

Well, in the first place, she was paid by the sponsor to give the seminars, and a large turnout assured her of future bookings by that sponsor. Plus she sold 120 copies of her self-published book, *Ten Ways to Super Memory*, to those attending the original seminar and approximately the same number of copies at the second seminar.

On top of that, the management at two retirement homes saw the newspaper item and hired her to give a six-hour seminar on the same subject at both of their establishments for a fee of $1,000 each. At these subsequent speaking engagements, she sold more books.

And all this came from writing just one news release that showed how the public could benefit.

But you may be thinking, "I don't know how my product (or service) will benefit the public."

Ask yourself these questions. Will it make someone healthier, smarter, safer, more relaxed, more comfortable, more stylish? Will it help people make money, get their teenagers to pay attention to them, or get their in-laws off their backs? Will it give them a better chance at romance or happiness? Will it entertain them or make them laugh? Will it touch their hearts in some way?

Your product or service has to be of some benefit to someone or else you have nothing to sell and certainly nothing worth publicizing.

But don't think monetary gain is the only reason for wanting to promote a product, service, or event. The truth is there are probably as many reasons as there are events. In fact, the motivation is sometimes quite altruistic.

The next news release (page 23) on the Sixth Annual Martin Luther King, Jr. Honors Banquet is a good example.

Dorothy Johnson, one of the organizers of the event, explained, "We wanted to present positive role models for young African Americans in our area."

The news release generated an article in the *Southwest Times Record*, Fort Smith, Arkansas and gave the committe valuable publicity.

Another example of a promotion not motivated by monetary gain is a letter written by David Alexander, program director at radio station KKHT-FM, Springfield, Missouri. Although not *technically* a news release, the letter acted as a news release announcing a record containing a new song by Scott Innes and his son. The letter explains the motivation for writing the song and tells how the record came to be made. The letter appears on page 24.

Since our troops had just started fighting in the Persian Gulf at the time, and millions of people had loved ones for whom they were longing and praying, the song struck a chord in many hearts. Soon it was being played on radio stations hundreds of miles away, not only in Missouri, but in the surrounding states.

Then newspapers across the state picked up the story. Page 25 shows one such article written by Cindy Paarman of the *Daily American Republic*, Poplar Bluff, Missouri.

The letter was used to inform the media of the record, so it acted as a news release. And it contained the criteria for which Paarman looks.

Dorothy J. Johnson
General Chairman
2034 No. 13th St.
Ft. Smith, AR 72904

MARTIN LUTHER KING, JR.
FEDERAL HOLIDAY PLANNING COMMITTEE
FT. SMITH, VAN BUREN & VICINITY

January 10, 1991

## MRS. ARKANSAS 1990 TO SPEAK!!

The Martin Luther King, Jr. Federal Holiday Planning Committee will present Mrs. Gail McLaughlin as the banquet speaker at their annual holiday banquet, Saturday, January 19, 1991, at the Sheraton Inn, 5711 Rogers Avenue, Fort Smith at 7:30 p.m.

Mrs. McLaughlin is the first African American to win the coveted title of Mrs. Arkansas in the State of Arkansas and serves as a role model.

Mrs. McLaughlin spent one month in the Soviet Union during the Mrs. America 1990 competition. She has received many awards that went along with the trip such as side visits and interviews with the people in Moscow, Leningrad and Pusca Village.

Tickets for this annual affair may be purchased from any of the committee members. The public is welcome.

CONTACT:

Ms. Euba Harris-Winton
783-4214

Mrs. Dorothy Johnson
782-4629

K K H T  9 8. 7

January 17, 1991

Dear Program Director:

The other day we received a letter in the mail from a woman
here in Springfield who has a four year old boy.  This boys
father is on the front line in the Persian Gulf.  The woman
stated that she helped her son write the letter to send to
his father who has been in the Persian Gulf since November.

The letter was so moving and touching that she made us a copy
of the letter to possibly read on the air and dedicate it to
the men and women fighting in the Persian Gulf who have
little ones back home in the United States.  I found the
letter to be overwhelming myself and gave it to my new
morning man, Scott Innes, to read on the air.  Scott had a
better idea, and his idea has become the most requested song
on 99 Hit FM.

We have been contacted by other stations and media sources
about the song and have made many dubs for other radio
stations, and we are talking with the local ABC TV affiliate
about putting video to the song.

Please find enclosed a copy of "Dear Daddy: The Wind Beneath
My Wings".  Give it a spin and the phones will go crazy.  For
further information, contact:

Dave Alexander
Program Director
99 Hit FM
883-9000

Sincerely

Dave Alexander,
Program Director

Note:  a copy of the song is available without the news bits.

# Disc Jockey, Son Record Wartime Song Based On Letter

By CINDY PAARMAN
DAR Staff Writer

Former Poplar Bluffian Scott Innes, now a Springfield disc jockey, has combined an anonymous idea and a highly requested song, focusing the two on wartime. The result is daily growing nationwide.

The idea stems from an anonymous letter sent to KKHT, 98.5 FM where Innes works. A Woman and her 4-year-old son wrote a letter to the boy's father, who is serving in the Persian Gulf.

Innes decided to have his own son, Josh, 4, read passages from the letter, mixing them with Bette Midler's hit song, "Wind Beneath My Wings." The song is titled, "Dear Daddy: Wind Beneath My Wings," and is now being aired over 400 radio stations across the country, including LKID and KJEZ in Poplar Bluff.

KLID began playing the song on Monday, Jan. 21, and it is being "well received," according to Sunny Skidmore, program director.

"I've always liked the song ("Wind Beneath My Wings")," Innes said. "It's very emotional itself and gets a lot of requests."

The song, he said, is also being put to video through the ABC television station, KSPR in Springfield, and may be sent by satellite to all ABC affiliates. The video will also be sent to VH1 (Video Hits 1), CMT (Coun-

**Josh Innes**
. . *read passages from letter.*

try Music Television), and MTV (Music Television).

Innes and his son will be presented with a courtesy resolution by the Missouri Senate on Feb. 5 in Jefferson City in recognition of their tribute to the soldiers involved in Operation Desert Storm. They will be guests in the Senate that day and will attend the sixth annual Governor's Cup Basketball game that evening.

Innes and his wife, Tammy, moved to Springfield from Poplar Bluff with their son this week.

material that would never make it into print."

Not only did Alexander's letter meet those standards, but lots of news values were involved, which gave the story "reader appeal."

1) Operation Desert Storm was on everyone's mind. (News value of timeliness.)

2) Scott Innes was a disc jockey, which gave him a degree of public recognition. (News value of prominence.)

3) He and his family had just moved from Poplar Bluff, so what he had done was of interest to readers in that city. (News value of proximity.)

4) The Missouri Senate was going to present Innes and his son a courtesy resolution in the state capitol in recognition of their tribute to the soldiers of Operation Desert Storm. (News value of eminence.)

5) The song itself touched peoples' hearts. (News value of human interest.)

Although monetary reward had not been the motivating factor for making the record, sales increased by approximately twenty percent after it was so widely publicized.

So, if your news release shows how it will benefit the public (i.e., touch their hearts or give them information in which they are interested), your product, service, or event has the best chance of being publicized.

The news releases shown in this chapter all contained news values. The next chapter shows how to get news values into your news release in order to make your story newsworthy.

Paarman says, "What I look for first in a news release are the basic who, what, when, where and why. After that, a little background is good. Most importantly, no matter what the content, I look for the name and telephone number for a contact. Without those, we could lose good

# CHAPTER 3

# NEWS VALUES

There are three major reasons why the media may not use the information from a news release: (1) It was received too late; (2) there is simply not enough space/time to work it into the publication or broadcast; or (3) it is not considered to be newsworthy.

Conflicts and disasters tend to get the majority of attention in all media. But, if you think about it, that's understandable.

If you have two children, and Margie tries to tell you she won a good citizenship award just as Herman runs into the room with blood streaming from his head, who is going to get your attention?

Right! Blood always gets attention.

Therefore, it's easy to see why Herman's bleeding head gets more attention than Margie's good citizenship award.

Yet, if Margie really wants attention, she will rush over to Herman, grab the scarf from around her neck, and quickly wrap it around Herman's throat. The next day's headlines will read, "GOOD CITIZENSHIP AWARD WINNER KILLS BROTHER IN MISPLACED TOURNIQUET APPLICATION."

But there are ways of getting space in newspapers short of committing murder.

For starters, remember that news is presented in units. Newspapers are divided into sections; TV news is divided into time segments.

You are not trying to compete for space in the front section. Your item does not have to be more riveting than front page world events. It just has to ace out the news about a new bank branch opening, the art association's fund-raiser, or someone's 90th birthday party.

That's not always easy to do, but it does cut the problem down to size.

People untrained in getting publicity often forget to ask themselves one very important question: *What's new*?

Is your business taking on a new partner? Is it moving to a new location? Is it coming out with a new product?

Is your club installing a new slate of officers? Is it offering a new bus trip to Las Vegas or Atlantic City as a fund-raiser?

As a family entertainer, have you developed a new act with new gimmics?

Is your church sending new missionaries to new locations?

Keep in mind: You can't take the "new" out of news, and old news isn't news at all...it's history.

A columnist friend of mine told me how upset a gentleman was when he found out that her newspaper was not going to do a feature story on his and his wife's sixtieth wedding anniversary, but that the event was only going to be mentioned as one item among many in her column.

The couple had owned a popular restaurant and bar thirty years ago, a place where many county residents had first met their future spouses. The gentleman felt this was newsworthy.

It was...to a limited extent. But it was only worth mentioning, not featuring. Since the name of the business had been changed when it was sold two decades ago and the area's population had quadrupled, most current residents would not even recognize the name of his old establishment.

Had the couple still owned the place and invited all who had found love there to attend their sixtieth anniversary party, that might very well have warranted a good size feature story. If the party took place around Valentine's Day, that would have made it even more newsworthy. But that was not the case.

Therefore, the only thing new was the fact that he and his wife were celebrating their sixtieth anniversary. While both laudable and enviable, that would not warrant a feature story.

So, you can see that focusing on *what's new* is the first step toward getting publicity.

Your next question should be, "What *news values* are involved?"

News values were mentioned briefly in the last chapter. But if you don't understand what the term "news values" means, don't let it throw you. News values are merely the qualifications or characteristics of news. The news values that editors look for in a newsworthy release are:

Conflict
Progress and Disaster
Consequence
Eminence and Prominence
Timeliness and Proximity
Novelty
Human Interest
Sex and Romance

There are many examples of actual news releases shown in this book that are much more exciting than the ones you are about to see. But for the purpose of illustrating how each news value can be used, I have intentionally chosen an organization and an event that are *not* particularly exciting: the mythical Bergtown Gardening Club and its installation luncheon.

If you can come to understand how news values are used in publicizing a rather mundane event, then a business, product or service that has some sparkle to it will be easy for you to write about.

## CONFLICT

The first news value is *conflict*.

Obviously, wars, murders, and political clashes are news. These kinds of conflicts have the potential of affecting the community at large, whether it is the local community or the world community. But a fistfight between two nine-year-old boys in the school yard, while it is conflict, is not news, because (1) it happens too often to be unusual and (2) only a handful of people are affected, namely the nine-year-old boys.

On the other hand, if their fathers, angry because of their children's fight, start a brawl at a city council meeting, that would probably get news coverage.

A take-over battle between corporate executives of multimillion dollar firms is news if the outcome could affect a large segment of the local, world, or business communities. But an individual's sale of a small diner after owning it for only two years is ordinarily not news because that would not significantly affect the community.

However, if it is the only diner within ten miles and the new owner is going to turn it into a soup kitchen for the poor, that would be news. Where would the local people go for lunch?

Beginning to get the idea?

But how could conflict be incorporated into a news release for a gardening club installation luncheon?

An installation luncheon is a difficult event to which to add "zing." But how about the example on page 29?

Obviously, the fight is on. How could the Old Town Blooming Idiots turn down such a challenge?

Additionally, the news release may pique an editor's interest because of two words: "unusual" (a red flag for most editors) and "epiphyllums." Unless the particular editor receiving this news release is a secret horticultural buff and just happens to know that epiphyllums are orchid cacti, the editor will have to look it up.

If the editor's curiosity has been tweaked to have invested that much time, the editor may send someone to cover the event. A photographer might also be sent because prize-winning epiphyllums would have visual appeal.

But to make sure an editor knows you would like a reporter to attend and that you are not merely looking for a notice in the "upcoming events" or "community calendar" section, you would send a short cover letter along with the news release.

Your cover letter should be typed on letterhead stationery, if possible, and might read like the example on page 30.

## PROGRESS AND DISASTER

The next news values in order of importance are *progress* and *disaster*. A new drug to cure cancer would be *progress* and definitely newsworthy. However, if the drug had been on the market for a few years and was found to cause birth defects in the children of women who have taken it, this would be a *disaster*. Again, the drug becomes newsworthy.

The news values of progress and disaster could be incorporated into the Bergtown Gardening Club's news release like the one on page 31.

In this example, you have mentioned something new...the chemical "dyfungi," and told of the progress being made in curing the disaster of fungus-riddled epiphyllums.

If you aren't a gardener, that might not seem like a big deal to you. But gardeners read news about gardening clubs and if there were such a chemical (I just made up the name), gardeners would be interested. And, if readers would be interested, then an editor will be interested.

## CONSEQUENCE

When Iraqi dictator Saddam Hussein's military invaded Kuwait, many nations responded by sending troops into Saudi Arabia in order to restrain him from further aggression. Their response was not only out of concern for the citizens of the Middle East, but for the possible *consequence* of global economic ruin if Hussein should gain control of all the oil fields in that area of the world.

For months, while the diplomatic avenues were explored and embargoes were established, no battles were fought. But, because the situation was such a powder keg, the media carried stories revolving around consequences.

**BERGTOWN GARDENING CLUB**
**233 Hollyhock Avenue**
**Bergtown, CA 90001**

FOR IMMEDIATE RELEASE                              CONTACT: Lily White
                                                  Telephone: 555-1001
Date: April 22, 2005

Installation Luncheon


            GAUNTLET TO BE THROWN AT GARDENING CLUB LUNCHEON


A challenge will be issued by the new officers of the Bergtown
Gardening Club at their installation luncheon to be held at 12:30
p.m., Friday, May 15, at the Midtown Restaurant, located at 1222
Ocean Blvd., Bergtown.


"We are tossing down the gauntlet, or in this case, the gardening
glove, and challenging the Old Town Blooming Idiots to a contest to
see which club can raise the largest epiphyllum in the next twelve
months," said Mary Gold, president-elect.


Some unusual, prize-winning epiphyllums will be on display at the
installation luncheon as examples of the type of competition the
Old Town Blooming Idiots will face.


Names of officers to be installed are as follow:  Mary Gold, president; Holly Green, vice-president; Rose Bush, secretary; and Susan
I. Black, treasurer.


For further information, contact Lily White at 555-1001.


                                ###

*News release using <u>conflict</u> as the primary news value.*

**BERGTOWN GARDENING CLUB**
**233 Hollyhock Avenue**
**Bergtown, CA 90001**

April 21, 2005

Ms. Harriet McCall
Social Editor
Bergtown Tribune
200 Main Street
Bergtown, CA 90001

Dear Ms. McCall:

Enclosed is a news release covering the upcoming installation luncheon
of the Bergtown Gardening Club.

We would welcome a reporter and/or a photographer to the event and would
like to have the press personnel to be our guest(s) for lunch.

If someone from your paper will be attending, please call me at 555-
1001 to let me know if a fish or chicken dish is preferred.

Sincerely,

Lily White
Publicity Chairwoman

*Sample cover letter...*

**BERGTOWN GARDENING CLUB**
**233 Hollyhock Avenue**
**Bergtown, CA 90001**


FOR IMMEDIATE RELEASE                          CONTACT: Lily White
                                               Telephone: 555-1001
Date: April 22, 2005


Installation Luncheon


NEW FUNGICIDE TO BE REVIEWED AT GARDENING CLUB LUNCHEON


Progress is being made in curing fungus infections which have
recently been destroying the epiphyllums in our area.  New methods
of combating this problem will be reviewed at the installation
luncheon of the Bergtown Gardening Club, to be held at 12:30 p.m.,
Friday, May 15, at the Midtown Restaurant, located at 1222 Ocean
Blvd., Bergtown.


President-elect Mary Gold will talk on "Saving Your Epiphyllums,"
and the use of the new chemical "dyfungi," which has drastically
reduced the ratio of fungus infections in specimens across the
country.


Names of officers to be installed are as follow: Mary Gold, president;  Holly Green, vice-president;  Rose Bush, secretary;  and
Susan I. Black, treasurer.


For further information, contact Lily White at 555-1001.


### 

*News release using* progress *and* disaster *as primary news values.*

All the stories were not of worldwide or far-reaching consequences. Many centered around local consequences. For instance, in our area, with its many military bases, we heard stories of how many marines and sailors had "moonlighted" at part-time jobs and how their shipping out had left some businesses scrambling to find replacement workers. There were also stories about children left with grandparents because both the mother and father were sent overseas. Even the Humane Society received a large number of pets because their owners were shipped out. All of these things were consequences of the Middle East crisis, before a bomb was dropped or a shot fired.

But many events not nearly as crucial as war in the Middle East can have significant consequences. The superintendent of schools in a nearby town recently spent the night on top of the elementary school as a consequence of challenging the students to read 2,500 books in a month. They did it, and up he went into his tent on top of the school building. However, he did not have to worry about getting hungry, for the children and their parents had supplied him with enough cookies and candy that the consequence of eating everything provided would have been a very upset stomach.

If a factory closes, the big story is usually the consequence of so many people losing their jobs. The real estate market may take a nose dive as a consequence of such vast unemployment. New car sales will plummet as a consequence.

On a cheerier note, business sales can skyrocket as a consequence of a *new* line of merchandise that is especially appealing. Homes can use less heating fuel as a consequence of a new method of insulation. Everyone would want to know about that one.

All of the above examples have the elements necessary for a newsworthy story.

An example of how the Bergtown Gardening Club might incorporate the news value of consequence into their news release is shown on page 33.

This release may be reaching a bit, but an epiphyllum display that could have the consequence of becoming a "prickly situation" might get coverage by a newspaper. After all, you are not trying to write Pulitzer Prize-winning prose. You are trying to get attention.

You can bet that if one of the guests did back into an epiphyllum and sued the club as a consequence, that story would hit the newspapers. That, of course, is not the kind of publicity you want, but it does illustrate the news value of consequence.

## EMINENCE AND PROMINENCE

This probably does not need much of an explanation. The fact is that big names make big news.

The opening of a small business or a church social might not be very newsworthy. But if a popular Hollywood hunk is a friend of the business owner and is coming to town for the opening, it would make the newspapers and probably be carried on the local TV and radio stations as well. If a nationally known TV evangelist were attending the church social, that too would get coverage.

So, if the Bergtown Gardening Club can do a little name dropping, the news values of *eminence* and *prominence* may very well get coverage for its installation luncheon.

Its news release might look like the one on page 34.

People love to read about other people who are "special" in some way. If Mary Gold has received kind words for her epiphyllums from the President of the United States, the editor quite likely will be interested in the event because he or she will wonder how it happened that the President knew about Gold's epiphyllums in the first place. Is she a personal friend of the first family? Or is the president a closet epiphyllum grower?

**BERGTOWN GARDENING CLUB**
**233 Hollyhock Avenue**
**Bergtown, CA 90001**

FOR IMMEDIATE RELEASE                    CONTACT: Lily White
                                         Telephone: 555-1001

Date: April 22, 2005

Installation Luncheon

SHOW OF EPIPHYLLUMS COULD BE PRICKLY SITUATION

Those attending the Bergtown Gardening Club's installation luncheon could get stuck with more than the bill.  Fifteen members will
display their epiphyllums at the luncheon, and that could turn
into a prickly situation unless the aisles between the displays
are wide.

President-elect Mary Gold said, "It will be the largest epiphyllum
display in Bergtown's history.  But members and guests will have
to watch their step, for backing into an epiphyllum can give one
quite a surprise."

The luncheon will be held at 12:30 p.m., on Friday, May 15, at the
Midtown Restaurant, located at 1222 Ocean Blvd., Bergtown.

Names of officers to be installed are as follow:  Mary Gold,
president; Holly Green, vice-president; Rose Bush, secretary; and
Susan I. Black, treasurer.

For further information, contact Lily White at 555-1001.

### 

*News release using* consequence *as the primary news value.*

**BERGTOWN GARDENING CLUB**
**233 Hollyhock Avenue**
**Bergtown, CA 90001**

FOR IMMEDIATE RELEASE                    CONTACT: Lily White
                                         Telephone: 555-1001
Date: April 22, 2005


Installation Luncheon


                    MAYOR TO PRESENT AWARD AT
                 BERGTOWN GARDENING CLUB LUNCHEON


Mayor Thornton Rosenbloom and his wife, Iris, both avid gardeners,
will be on hand for the installation luncheon of the Bergtown
Gardening Club, to be held at 12:30 p.m., on Friday, May 15, at
the Midtown Restaurant, located at 1222 Ocean Blvd., Bergtown.

The mayor will present the Golden Gardening Glove Award to president-elect Mary Gold, who has been lauded as the "best epiphyllum
grower in the world" by the President of the United States.

Names of officers to be installed are as follow:  Mary Gold,
president; Holly Green, vice-president; Rose Bush, secretary; and
Susan I. Black, treasurer.

For further information, contact Lily White at 555-1001.


                            ###

*News release using* eminence *and* prominence *as primary news values.*

And, if Mayor "Thorny" Rosenbloom is popular, the editor will report on his activities because the readers want to know what he's up to.

## TIMELINESS AND PROXIMITY

These news values are useful in measuring the newsworthiness of an event.

Remember the couple who had owned the restaurant/bar, mentioned earlier in this chapter? If the establishment had been sold just the week before the couple's sixtieth wedding anniversary in order to finance a worldwide cruise to celebrate their anniversary, this could have been a feature story about a popular place changing hands and what was to become of the owners. That would make it a *timely* story for the local paper (although many papers shy away from stories announcing when people will be away from home for extended periods, for such information could make their homes easy targets for burglary). However, it would *not* make a good story for a newspaper 200 miles away because of a lack of *proximity*.

Working timeliness and proximity into a gardening club news release for an installation luncheon is a tough proposition, but the example on page 36 is a good attempt.

Speaking of May planting in May would be timely. Also, it's obvious that Mary Gold is not just any garden-variety garden club president. Although she is a longtime resident of Bergtown (proximity), Mary is a "with it" lady jet-setter who knows something about the Middle East, which is perennially in the news. And if the luncheon is occurring at approximately the same time as a summit concerning the Middle East, it would add even more news value to the installation, for her talk would be especially timely.

To capture the aspects of timeliness and proximity, try to connect what you wish to publicize with something that is pertinent to your area at this particular time or something that is currently headline news.

For example, one restaurant in our town had an Easter egg contest the week before Easter with local celebrities as judges. A retirement home had a Valentine's Ball. Many churches have Christmas pageants every year. These are obvious chances to work timeliness into a news release. But there are other opportunities as well. Throughout the year, there are weeks devoted to celebrating various things, such as National Secretaries' Week, National Clown Week, or National Disabled Persons' Week. Libraries carry books such as *Chase's Annual Events*, listing a surprising array of designated days, weeks, and months.

For example, in January there is the "National Prunes for Breakfast Week," and "National Oatmeal Week," to name but a few. With as many topics as are listed, you are quite likely to find a designated day or week that is somehow related to what you want to publicize.

## NOVELTY

If something is really unusual or different, it's news. Complaining to your congressman is not news. But an eighty-year-old woman who hitchhiked from California to Washington, D.C., to register her complaint in person to her congressman did make news. (Of course, a congressman is going to find time to see an eighty-year-old woman who hitchhikes that distance. Think of the consequences of negative news coverage if he didn't.)

An artist making wood sculptures is not usually news, but if he does it with a nine-pound chainsaw, that's news.

Certainly green beans and onions are not usually newsworthy, but foot-long green beans and two-pound onions measuring ten inches in diameter are news.

**BERGTOWN GARDENING CLUB**
**233 Hollyhock Avenue**
**Bergtown, CA 90001**

FOR IMMEDIATE RELEASE              CONTACT: Lily White
                                        Telephone: 555-1001

Date: April 22, 2005

Installation Luncheon

PRESIDENT-ELECT WILL ANSWER QUESTION,
"IS MAY TOO LATE TO PLANT FOR FALL BLOOMS?"
AND DISCUSS GARDENS OF CAIRO, EGYPT

Mary Gold will be installed as president of the Bergtown Gardening Club at a luncheon to be held at 12:30 p.m., on Friday, May 15, at the Midtown Restaurant, located at 1222 Ocean Blvd., Bergtown.

Gold, a resident of Bergtown for 30 years, recently returned from Egypt where she toured some of Cairo's most beautiful gardens. Following her inaugural speech, Gold will discuss Cairo's gardens and why the epiphyllum will never replace eggplant as the favorite flowering plant in Middle East countries and cultures. She will also give tips on May planting for fall blooms.

Names of officers to be installed are as follow: Mary Gold, president; Holly Green, vice-president; Rose Bush, secretary; and Susan I. Black, treasurer.

For further information, contact Lily White at 555-1001.

###

*News release using* timeliness *and* proximity *as primary news values.*

If the Bergtown Gardening Club can come up with something novel to put in its news release, it might catch an editor's attention.

How about the release on page 38?

Novelty always draws attention. Humans are curious beasts, and no one is more curious than an editor. The fact that these plants are not grown by just anyone might be the "something different" that catches the editor's eye.

## HUMAN INTEREST

We have all seen stories about families being reunited after thirty years or about a dog who saved his master's life. Technically, since most human interest stories are a combination of other news values, many experts do not consider *human interest* as a news value in itself, but rather a story value.

However, the Bergtown Gardening Club might include human interest in its news release like the one on page 39.

## SEX AND ROMANCE

This does not need an explanation. If a senator is seen cavorting with an exotic dancer or a political candidate is caught in a cozy weekend hideaway with a woman other than his wife, it's news. From the days of old, when every royal court buzzed with news of who was doing what to whom, sex and romance have been considered newsworthy. Ancient drawings and statuary are graphic examples of how long sex has been of interest to all people in all cultures throughout time.

The Bergtown Garden club might incorporate sex into its news release like the example on page 40.

So, there you have it. We have gone through examples using each of the news values. You now have a general idea of how you might incorporate news values into your own news releases.

Notice I have used the term "news" release rather than "press" release. For one thing, your news release may be going to TV and radio stations...not just to newspapers. But more significantly, by calling it "news" release, you will get used to the idea that there must be news in a news release.

Did you also notice the format used in the preceding examples of news releases? All of the samples had FOR IMMEDIATE RELEASE shown at the top, along with the date the news release was sent. Plenty of lead time was allowed.

Of course, if all you want is a listing in the "Upcoming Events" section, you would use the words: COMMUNITY CALENDAR LISTING.

Your news release is like a mini-story in itself. The information shown in your news release and your cover letter tells the media what you wish done with the mini-story.

You may have also noticed that the news releases contained quotes from president-elect Mary Gold and others. Try to use quotes in your news releases whenever it is appropriate. Quotes make releases more interesting and the reporters' jobs easier, for they are armed with ready-made quotations for their stories. However, avoid quoting ordinary statements, such as, "I was pleased to be elected." Aim for a quote that indicates the character of the person speaking or has some news value of its own, such as, "If my opponent had not stuffed the ballot box, I would have been elected two years ago." That should get everyone's attention.

From studying the preceding examples, you should now have a better idea of how to write a news release that emphasizes the most newsworthy aspect of an event in order to capture an editor's attention.

Do you think the editor receiving the news release from the Bergtown Gardening Club

**BERGTOWN GARDENING CLUB**
**233 Hollyhock Avenue**
**Bergtown, CA 90001**

FOR IMMEDIATE RELEASE                    CONTACT: Lily White
                                         Telephone: 555-1001

Date: April 22, 2005

Installation Luncheon


RARE EPIPHYLLUMS TO BE DISPLAYED AT LUNCHEON


"Despite the enthusiasm for house plants which has swept the country in the last 15 years, only one person in 1,000 even tries to grow epiphyllums," said Mary Gold, president-elect of the Bergtown Gardening Club.


In an effort to popularize this rare species, free epiphyllums will be given to each person attending the luncheon.  Gold will talk on the care and feeding of epiphyllums, which she says are "sometimes temperamental, but worth the effort."


The new slate of officers will be installed at a luncheon to be held at 12:30 p.m., on Friday, May 15, at the Midtown Restaurant, located at 1222 Ocean Blvd., Bergtown.


Names of officers to be installed are as follow:  Mary Gold, president; Holly Green, vice-president; Rose Bush, secretary; and Susan I. Black, treasurer.


For further information, contact Lily White at 555-1001


###

*News release using* novelty *as the primary news value.*

**BERGTOWN GARDENING CLUB**
**233 Hollyhock Avenue**
**Bergtown, CA 90001**

FOR IMMEDIATE RELEASE                    CONTACT: Lily White
                                         Telephone: 555-1001
Date: April 22, 2005

Installation Luncheon

OLDEST ROSE RECIPIENT TO BE HONORED

The Bergtown Gardening Club, which provides roses and other cut
flowers weekly to nursing homes in the area, will honor Pansy
Hawkins, the oldest local nursing home resident, at its installation luncheon to be held at 12:30 p.m., on Friday, May 15, at the
Midtown Restaurant, located at 1222 Ocean Blvd., Bergtown.

"Seeing those beautiful flowers just brightens my whole week",
said Hawkins, 99, a resident of Bergtown for 76 years.

Names of officers to be installed are as follow:  Mary Gold,
president; Holly Green, vice-president; Rose Bush, secretary; and
Susan I. Black, treasurer.

For further information, contact Lily White at 555-1001.

### 

*News release using* human interest *as the primary news value.*

**BERGTOWN GARDENING CLUB**
**233 Hollyhock Avenue**
**Bergtown, CA 90001**

FOR IMMEDIATE RELEASE                          CONTACT: Lily White
                                                Telephone: 555-1001
Date: April 22, 2005

Installation Luncheon

SEX EDUCATION IN THE GARDEN

"If you wish to teach your child about sex," says Mary Gold,
president-elect of the Bergtown Gardening Club, "you need to go no
farther than your garden or your greenhouse for examples."

Gold will speak on "Sex Education in the Garden" at the Bergtown
Gardening Club's installation luncheon to be held at 12:30 p.m.,
on Friday, May 15, at the Midtown Restaurant, located at 1222
Ocean Blvd., Gergtown.

Names of officers to be installed are as follow:  Mary Gold,
president; Holly Green, vice-president; Rose Bush, secretary; and
Susan I. Black, treasurer.

For further information, contact Lily White at 555-1001.

###

*News release using* sex *as the primary news value.*

will be disappointed when he or she finds out epiphyllums are orchid cacti rather than rare man-eating plants? Perhaps a tad, but not if a few of the members (or even one) have won prizes for their epiphyllums. And not if you make it plain that your club's main objective in the coming year is to promote epiphyllums to the point where there will be one in every pot...or potting shed, as the case may be.

Just as the reporter's aim is to grab the reader's attention, your aim is to grab the editor's attention by providing information that is newsworthy enough to interest his or her readers.

So, before you even start to compose your news release, stop and think about the list of news values and consider just what it is about your product, service, or event that is most newsworthy.

An editor looks forward to hearing from business people, publicity chairpersons, and others who have a "news sense" and who provide complete and newsworthy information in their news releases. So if you give editors what they need, you will have no problem getting coverage.

More tips on how to get coverage in print media are included in the next chapter.

## THE MEDIA NEEDS YOUR NEWS

All branches of the media compete with each other for audience attention. The better a station's ratings or the larger the circulation, the more advertising it gets and the more it can charge. After all, news reporting is a business, too, and the media is out to make a profit like any other business. And it is through advertising that the media makes its money. Therefore, they must report information that readers and listeners need and want to know.

Editors and program directors cannot get all the news they need from inside sources alone. To be competitive, they need your news releases to provide interesting stories and to inform them of what is happening locally.

The media has a limited amount of print space and airtime. For this reason they must choose information that will provide the most valuable information or best entertainment for the time and space available. Consequently they are very selective in what they use. Although most news releases are rejected, good releases are needed and welcomed.

# CHAPTER 4

# GETTING NEWSPAPER COVERAGE

Now that you have decided that you want and need publicity, it has probably occurred to you that you will be meeting and dealing with people who work for all branches of the media. Although I have emphasized getting publicity placed in print media (specifically newspapers), the same basic principles apply for all media. (The next chapter deals more specifically with getting coverage in electronic media—radio and television.)

A lot of people are awed by those who work in the media because they view them as "names" or even "celebrities." But media people have a job to do, just as accountants, lawyers, or truck drivers do. The difference is that media people need more input from outside sources than most other professions. That is where you come in.

No newspaper, newsletter, magazine, radio or television station has enough personnel to search out everything that is newsworthy. The front page material (or top of the TV or radio news) is, of course, gathered by staff people or comes from wire services.

But all news is not front page material. Wars, murders, rapes, and muggings usually go in the front section. But further back is the happier news, shown in the entertainment, social, and business sections. These sections may not carry material as sensational as the front page news, but items in these sections are of great interest to many readers, otherwise, a newspaper would not go to the expense of publishing them.

On the other hand, while newspapers may have reporters assigned permanently to the White House, the Pentagon, city hall, and the police station, no newspaper has enough manpower to send reporters to every business in town or to every club, lodge, church, or charitable organization to find out what is going on. These sections of a newspaper depend heavily on outside sources for information.

Your news release can be that outside source.

But, as noted earlier, editors complain that the majority of news releases they receive are usually terrible and get trashed immediately. The news releases either do not give the editors the complete facts they need, or the most important information is buried someplace near the bottom of the release rather than at the top where it belongs.

The practice of putting the most pertinent information at the beginning started during the Civil War. Reporters, in wiring their stories to their newspapers, never knew when a telegraph line would be cut or blown up. On the assumption that their transmission could be interrupted any second, they wired the information in descending order of importance. What started as an expediency became the norm.

Since this practice has been in effect for more than 130 years, editors sometimes assume that everyone knows it and, therefore, on an especially busy day, scan only the first few paragraphs of a news release to see if it is something in which they might be interested.

Many a good story has been lost because important information was buried at the bottom. But with the hundreds of letters and news releases editors receive each week, this information can easily be overlooked.

In today's fast-paced society, even the readers often scan only the first few paragraphs of a newspaper story, for they know the most important information is going to be at the top.

(Keep in mind that, because this "inverted pyramid" type of writing is commonplace, an editor usually cuts a story from the bottom up.)

By now, you may be thinking, "This is too much trouble. There are too many things to remember on how to keep my news release out of the trash. I'll just pop down to the newspaper and talk to the editor in person."

*Forget it!*

You can't just walk in to someone's office. Newspapers have reception areas, just like other businesses, and it is unlikely you will get in to see anyone without an appointment.

Granted, city rooms are no longer places where men sit at their desks, hats pushed to the back of their heads, while they puff on cigars and peck away at their typewriters, churning out hot news. (I saw the movie, "The Front Page," too!)

These days, you hear the soft hum of computers, you see "no smoking" signs on the wall, and there are as many women as men in the city room...and no one wears a hat at work anymore.

However, the sense of urgency involved in newspaper writing has not changed, and editors don't have time to mess with someone just walking in off the street wanting free publicity.

So, how *should* you do it?

First, you head for the public library for a look at the reference book *Finder Binder*. This book is published for various regions and lists all the newspapers and editors (as well as TV and radio stations and their personnel) located in your area.

Another excellent source in which to locate names and addresses of newspapers and other media is *Gale Directory of Publications and Broadcast Media.*

If you already know in which newspaper you want publicity, you can call and find out who handles the news section in which you wish to appear.

Once you have determined the name of the editor, write a brief, information-packed news release and send it with a cover letter to that editor's attention.

If you are writing about an event to which the public is invited, you will want an editor to run an advance notice. You would definitely want advance publicity on a new business opening, a church-sponsored fashion show, or your club's art exhibit, for such events depend on the public's attendance for their success.

The news release on page 44, although not done in the standard format, generated several newspaper stories which resulted in a good turnout for the publicized event. And, as you can see, this is one news release which did *not* prompt an editor to ask, "Where are these clowns coming from?"

It not only tells an editor where the clowns are coming from, but where they are going to be, when, why, and how they got there.

This news release was not done by a professional publicist (the majority of news

## SAN DIEGO STATE UNIVERSITY CLOWN CLUB
P.O. Box 151076 ● San Diego, CA 92115

```
DATE:    3 MARCH 1987              SUBJECT:  CLOWN ON PARADE
CONTACT: SANDY JAY, PUBLICITY CHAIRMAN - 236-1946
         DEE GEE, CONVENTION CHAIRMAN - 223-1138
```

San Diego State University (SDSU) Clown Club will present PARADE-ABILITY, a World Clown Association (WCA) convention competition, at Seaport Village, on April 11th, at 10:30 A.M., for the review and judging of clowns (over 500 are expected) as they appear in costume and perform with parade props. These activities are not just for the hundreds of clowns parading, but for all San Diegans to see and enjoy, so come join them.

As the clowns are assembling for the parade they will work together to create the world's longest balloon animal, to be entered into the Guinness Book of World Records.

When the SDSU Clown Club members attended the Third Annual WCA Convention in Las Vegas in 1985, they as a club and individuals, walked away with seven (7) trophies for skits and other competitions, more than any other club attending the convention. The club also won the bid to host the Fifth Annual WCA Convention here in San Diego.

In addition, the SDSU Clown Club will host Ringling Bros Clown College auditions as part of their activities for the Fifth Annual WCA Convention, between April 7 through April 12. The convention is a closed convention for clowns only throughout the USA, Canada, and other foreign ports, but the auditions are open to anyone desiring to become a circus clown, for information call Sandy Jay, 236-1946.

# Clowns to compete here

San Diego State University (SDSU) Clown Club will present PARADE-ABILITY, a World Clown Association (WCA) convention competition, at Seaport Village, on April 11th at 10:30 a.m., for the review and judging of clowns (over 500 are expected) as they appear in costume and perform with parade props. These activities are not just for the hundreds of clowns parading, but for all San Diegans to see and enjoy, so come join them.

As the clowns are assembling for the parade, they will work together to create the world's longest balloon animal, to be entered into the Guinness Book of World Records.

When the SDSU Clown Club members attended the Third Annual WCA Convention in Las Vegas in 1985, they as a club and individuals, walked away with seven trophies for skits and other competitions, more than any other club attending the convention. The club also won the bid to host the fifth annual WCA Convention here in San Diego.

In addition, the SDSU Clown Club will host Ringling Bros. Clown College auditions as part of their activities for the fifth annual WCA Convention, between April 7 through April 12. The convention is a closed convention for clowns only throughout the USA, Canada, and other foreign ports, but the auditions are open to anyone desiring to become a circus clown. For information, call Sandy Jay, 236-1946.

**Saturday, April 11**
**Clown Paradability.** World Clown Association competition gets underway 10:30 a.m. at Seaport Village, with up to 500 clowns parading, performing antics, and in general, clowning around. They will also attempt to create the world's longest balloon animal. Free. 236-1946.

*Newspaper article (left), calendar listing (above), magazine feature article (top of next page), and after-the-fact coverage (bottom of next page), all resulted from the same news release.*

releases received by a newspaper aren't from professional publicists). But it was effective. It contained the Five W's: Who, What, When, Where, and Why. *And it listed telephone numbers for the contact persons* in case additional information was needed.

Because it contained such good and complete information right from the start, it was used almost verbatim in the above story in *The Valley Voice*, a San Diego, California, publication.

Do you think the editor of *The Valley Voice* cared if the news release was done by a professional publicist or even if it had minor technical flaws? I doubt it. I think the editor was probably delighted that it contained information of interest to readers and could be run without many changes.

The same news release was also sent to other San Diego publications. One of them, *Uptown*, ran the small calendar listing in its April issue.

In addition to the calendar listing it had run in April, *Uptown* also carried after-the-fact coverage in its May issue. There was a picture of the event on its front page, and further back was an extensive pictorial display.

Another, *San Diego Metropolitan*, ran a full page story in advance of the event.

No need to tell you that the publicity worked well in drawing a large crowd to the event—you can see for yourself.

Although the clowns volunteered their time and services that day, many were noticed by potential customers and several obtained future paid bookings as a result of the exposure.

*HERE COME THE CLOWNS*

# A Colossal Cluster Of Clowns

by **Trish Clenney Brown**

If one clown can warm the cockles of your heart, imagine that sensation multiplied by 500. Watch out for spontaneous combustion on April 11.

That Saturday at 10:30 a.m. hundreds of clowns will converge on Seaport Village, romping, cavorting and parading in an event called "Parade-ability" which is part of the fifth annual World Clown Association Convention held this year for the first time in San Diego. Since most of the convention activities are for members only, Parade-ability offers a chance for the rest of us to see

this astonishing conclave of clowns prance around Seaport Village in all their costumed hilarity.

Clowns from all over the United States, as well as Canada, Mexico, Germany, England, Italy, Switzerland and Panama, will compete in a costume and parade prop contest. At the same time, they'll cooperate to make the world's longest balloon animal; figure about a foot and a half of balloon to each clown, multiply by 500 and you've got one very long animal. Later, the grease-painted battalion will

treat onlookers to a kazoo concert.

One of the contest's judges will be Annette Little, owner of the Seaport Village shop **Here Come the Clowns.** Little, a sculptor and painter, began creating clown figures 20 years ago. After that, starting the store came as a natural extension of her fascination.

"Clowns seem to touch people in a way that nothing else can," says Little. She attributes this quality to the clown's ability to tap childhood memories of things beautiful and fun and to take you away from the

*Hundreds of such grease-painted jesters will soon converge on the village to practice the serious art of clowning.*

present moment to a more magical one.

Little's shop is filled with clowns: big and little clowns, funny and sad clowns, jesters, Pierrot dolls in their lovely satin costumes, Red Skelton

Jan Eastman—now Sandy Jay, the Sailor Clown and vice president of the SDSU club—got her start that way. She was working in sales when she heard about the clown club two and a half years ago. "First

## Just clownin' around

at **Seaport Village**

No joke! Hundreds of clowns came to town April 7-12, for the Fifth World Clown Association Convention...five days of exhaustive antics and competitions to find the best clown around.

At Seaport Village, they created the World's Longest Balloon Animal amid amused shoppers and kids who got caught up in their act!

*Photos by Marti Kranzberg*

So, if you, like the clown who wrote the preceding release, are a novice at writing news releases, don't be afraid that your news release may not be 100 percent technically perfect, as long as you have provided complete details. Of course you will want to write as well as possible, but don't let your fear or lack of experience keep you from sending a news release. Remember, an editor is looking for facts.

The preceding example shows how advance publicity can result in increased attendance at an event. However, at times drawing a crowd is not what you want from publicity. In fact, there are situations in which you would not want advance publicity at all, but would want a newspaper story to appear only after a certain date. If an event is not open to the public, advance publicity is not necessary and sometimes not even desirable. You would want only after-the-fact publicity.

Say, for instance, you own a small glass company that sells household and auto glass. You are going to throw a party on June 20, and invite some of your steady customers so they can see how your new line of mirror tiles have been used in your own home. In other words, your home will be your showcase. You can't afford to invite the general public, yet you would like for them to know about your new product line.

Of course, the easiest way to handle the situation would be to send the business or social editor an invitation to the party and hope that someone from the newspaper will be assigned to cover the event. The reporter would then write up a story after the party had taken place.

But you can't be sure that someone will be available to cover your party, and you really want to let the public know about it.

Under these circumstances, you would send your news release three weeks in advance of the affair, but you would use the release information line: "FOR RELEASE ON: June 21," the day *after* the party.

*Your news release would be written as though the party had already taken place.*

An example of this type of release is on the following two pages.

Such a news release could be used as the basis of a story without the press having to attend. However, sending this kind of news release does not prohibit you from inviting the press, just in case someone is available to cover the event. After all, such a lavish party would be a good public relations opportunity.

So, if you want the press to attend, you would also send a cover letter, such as the one on page 50.

The guest list alone should prompt an editor to attend or send a reporter (remember the news value of prominence?). But if the directions get lost, no one will show up. So *staple* the map to the letter.

You might want to send this news release to both the social editor and the business editor, so if one is not interested the other might be. But, if you do send it to both editors, *add a note at the bottom saying you have sent it to both editors.* By telling both editors that the other editor has also received an invitation and/or copy of your news release, they can decide which one will cover the event.

It is extremely annoying to arrive at an event and meet another reporter from your own newspaper who is there to cover the same event. This often occurs when someone "peppers," as it's called. In other words, just to make sure that an event will be covered, news releases about an event are sent to several different editors on the same newspaper. Although editors try to coordinate with each other, each one receives far too many pieces of information to clear everything with all the other editors. What seems interesting to one often seems interesting to another, and each will assign someone to cover the event without being aware that another editor is covering it.

## AAA GLASS COMPANY
### 12 Crystal Lane
### Bergtown, CA 90001

FOR RELEASE ON: June 21, 2005                    CONTACT:  John Smith
                                                 Telephone:  555-1335

Glass Products Inventory Expanded

PROMINENT GUESTS GET PREVIEW OF ETCHED MIRROR TILES

Prominent guests, from politicians to TV stars, saw themselves reflected in the best light at the soiree held at the home of John and Pamela Smith on June 20.

The Smiths used their home as a showcase for the new line of etched mirror tiles just added to the inventory of their business, AAA Glass Company, 12 Crystal Lane, Bergtown.

Among those on the guest list were State Senator Jim Marks, Mayor Horace Dunn, Councilwoman Elizabeth Jones, and the stars of the new TV sitcom "Sweethearts," Jack and Deidre Dey.  Deidre was Pam Smith's college roommate.

The 75 guests were given a tour of the Smith's home.  Two walls of their large living room are covered with the mirrored tiles, etched in an Oriental design to coordinate with the Far East theme used throughout the house and garden.  The decorative mirror tiles are also used in the five bedrooms and five baths, as well as in the poolside guest house.

- MORE -

*After-the-fact news release.*

Page 2   <u>Glass Products Inventory Expanded</u>

"It's marvelous how a few of these etched mirror tiles can spark up a room and make it seem larger," Smith said.  "Pamela and I felt that the best way to show this was to invite some of our customers and friends and let them see the results for themselves."

The guests, coiffured, bejeweled, and looking elegant in their evening attire, began the evening with hors d'oeuvres and cocktails around the pool.  At 9 p.m., a lavish buffet of French cuisine was served in the dining room.

Musical entertainment by the Tuneful Trio was offered throughout the evening.

For further information, please contact John Smith at 555-1335.

###

**AAA GLASS COMPANY**
**12 Crystal Lane**
**Bergtown, CA 90001**

June 1, 2005

Ms. Harriet McCall
Social Editor
Bergtown Tribune
200 Main Street
Bergtown, CA 90001

Dear Ms. McCall:

You are invited to attend the party described in the enclosed news release, which will be held at 7 p.m., Sat., June 20, at our home at 567 Nob Hill Dr., Bergtown.  A map to our home is attached.

Sincerely,


John Smith

R.S.V.P.

Dual scheduling occurs most often when an event is borderline between being a social event and a business or political event.

For example, once I was scheduled by my editor to cover a "Meet the Mayor" brunch, sponsored by a women's political organization. The publicity chairwoman sent news releases to both the social editor and the city editor. Each thought it was newsworthy. Each assigned a reporter. Both of us were surprised when we ran into each other at the doughnut table. And both were annoyed, because one of us could have slept late that Saturday morning, and each wished it had been she.

Naturally, when the reporters tell their editors about the dual coverage, the editors become very leery about sending anyone the next time they receive a news release from that person or organization.

"Peppering" is one of the fastest ways to irritate editors and make them less cooperative.

However, most events fall into more clear cut categories. For example, your club's installation luncheon is a social event, so you would contact the social editor. And, since such luncheons are usually private affairs, you would probably want only an after-the-fact write-up in the newspaper in order to let the public know about your organization, perhaps as a means of boosting your membership.

Your news release might look like the one on page 52.

If a reporter is not available to cover the event, the information that you have just provided could be used as the basis for an item on the Bergtown Gardening Club.

However, if you feel that you would receive more thorough coverage (maybe even get your picture on the social page) if someone from the newspaper attended, you can still invite the press.

Your cover letter might read like the one on the page 53.

You have just given yourself an entree to that editor, for if the editor does not call you within a week, what could be more reasonable than a follow-up call under those circumstances? If the editor seems a bit harried and short when you call, don't take it personally...it's most likely deadline pressure.

In fact, for the best reception by any editor, you should make it your business to find out which are the most convenient times to call. For instance, if you want to talk with someone who works for a newspaper that comes out in the morning, *do not* call in the afternoon, for he or she is working on tomorrow morning's copy. If it is an afternoon paper, *do not* call in the morning. Call after 2 p.m., after deadlines have been met.

Schedules differ from newspaper to newspaper and from department to department. Cheryl Hall, business editor for *The Dallas Morning News*, says she hates to get calls on Friday because she is trying to wrap up stories for the weekend editions. But Lizanne Poppins, editor of the home and garden section of *The San Diego Union*, prefers to get calls on Friday because her deadline for that week has passed.

So, make it easier on everyone and find out when is the best time to call. Then make your conversation brief and to the point.

Even if your event isn't covered, if you have had an opportunity to talk with the editor, you may establish a better working relationship for the future.

Above all, never be obnoxious or "pushy." Keep it polite, businesslike, and courteous. The editor will love you.

Incidentally, you may have noticed that the news releases for both the AAA Glass Company and the Bergtown Gardening Club were sent three weeks in advance of the event. This is necessary for scheduling purposes if you want the press to attend.

**BERGTOWN GARDENING CLUB**
**233 Hollyhock Avenue**
**Bergtown, CA 90001**

FOR RELEASE ON: May 16, 2005                    CONTACT: Lily White
                                                Telephone: 555-1001

Installation Luncheon

            BERGTOWN GARDENING CLUB'S NEW OFFICERS INSTALLED

Mary Gold began her second term as president of the Bergtown
Garden Club at its installation luncheon held Friday, May 15, at
the Midtown Restaurant in Bergtown.

The Bergtown Gardening Club was established in 1912 and is the
oldest gardening club in the city.  It has doubled its membership
in the past year under Gold's direction.

Other officers installed at the luncheon were Holly Green, vice
president; Rose Bush, secretary; and Susan I. Black, treasurer.

The Bergtown Gardening Club regularly meets at 2 p.m., the first
Tuesday of each month, at the Community Center, 841 Broadway,
Bergtown.  Prospective members are welcome.

Contact Lily White at 555-1001 for further information.

                            ###

*After-the-fact news release.*

**BERGTOWN GARDENING CLUB**
**233 Hollyhock Avenue**
**Bergtown, CA 90001**


April 21, 2005


Ms. Harriet McCall
Social Editor
Bergtown Tribune
200 Main Street
Bergtown, CA 90001

Dear Ms. McCall:

We would like for you or one of your reporters and/or a photographer to be our guests at the upcoming installation luncheon of the Bergtown Gardening Club.  It will be held at 12:30 p.m., Friday, May 15, at the Midtown Restaurant, 1222 Ocean Blvd., Bergtown.

However, in case press personnel are unable to attend, I have enclosed a news release on the event, which you may be able to use for an item about the Bergtown Gardening Club's installation luncheon after May 16.

If you or other newspaper personnel will be attending as our guest(s) for lunch, please call me at 555-1001 to let me know if a fish or chicken dish is preferred.

Sincerely,


Lily White
Publicity Chairwoman

It's amazing how many people call at the last minute and expect a reporter to run right over. But it usually doesn't work that way except for "hard news" stories.

Even if all you want is an item to appear in the "upcoming events" column, you must get the information to the newspaper two to three weeks in advance of when you wish the item to appear.

There are two reasons for that. One is that the "upcoming events" columns are usually done on a first-come, first-served basis. The second reason for such a long lead time is that the social, business, and entertainment pages are some of the first to go to the layout people. "Hard news" stories (wars, murders, rapes, and robberies, etc.) are done at the last minute. Obviously, the layout people can't do all of the pages in the last twelve hours before the newspaper hits the street.

And whatever you do, after you have sent your news release and/or a reporter has covered your event, *do not call the editor and ask when the item about your event will be run.*

Such calls are very annoying. It's time consuming and serves no real purpose, because often an editor does not know specifically when a particular item will appear. It depends on the space available, and the available space depends on how much advertising is included in an edition of the newspaper.

One aspect of the business that most people do not understand is that newspapers are often "zoned." This means that what appears in the social, business, and entertainment sections of newspapers delivered to one part of your city is not necessarily what appears in those sections of the newspapers delivered in another part of your city.

The reason for zoning has to do with advertising. Advertising rates are based on the number of people who will be exposed to your ad. The more expensive ads are in the front section of a newspaper, which is the same for all zones and, therefore, reaches the most people.

If you have a restaurant, a dress shop, or a small market on the north side of town, your potential customers most likely will be from within a ten to fifteen mile radius of your place of business. It would be a waste of your money to spend extra bucks to advertise in the zone for the south side of town. Therefore, by placing an ad in the business or lifestyle section for your zone only, you save money yet reach your potential customers.

For the same edition of a newspaper, advertising can be heavy in one zone and light in another. Because of this, an article may be run in full in one zone, but have several paragraphs chopped off in another. Or it may not appear at all. Or one zone may have room for more pictures than another zone.

I once got a call from a man who said, "A friend of mine just called and said he'd seen my picture in the paper. I get the same paper and I didn't see my picture."

The problem was that the two men did not actually get the "same" newspaper. His friend was in a different zone which had less advertising that day and, therefore, had room for his picture.

It is acceptable to ask the reporter at the time an event is being covered for an *approximate* date an article might appear. However, reporters can never be absolutely certain when or even if a piece will appear. The best way to make sure you don't miss the item is to read the newspaper every day until the article in which you are interested is published. Ask your friends in other zones if they will keep their eyes open also.

And don't be discouraged if you do not see the article within two or three weeks. Barbara Brabec, home business development specialist and author of *Creative Cash and Homemade Money*, tells of the time she sent a news release to a newspaper and heard nothing for three years. When the newspaper finally got around to doing a story on home-based businesses, her release was found in the reference file. She then received a call for an update interview, and an article was printed soon afterward.

A three-year delay between the time a newspaper receives a news release and a story is published is very unusual, unless, of course, the news release is one that says, "RELEASE AT WILL," which indicates that the information is good now, and will be good a month from now or a year from now. However, you never know if or when your release will be used. A news release that says, "RELEASE AT WILL," is sometimes tucked in a file and saved for an emergency. For instance, if a scheduled story does not come together for some reason and an editor is left with space to fill at the last minute, it helps to have a backup story on hand.

However, most news items are published within two to four weeks at the latest. And look on the bright side! By continuing to read the newspaper while you wait for your article to appear, you will become very well informed on everything that is going on in your community. You might even pick up some new ideas by reading what others are doing. And that can't be all bad.

The examples used in this chapter covered the kinds of events you might see in your own local newspaper. They had appeal for a certain audience. But, with the exception of the San Diego State University's Parade-Ability, they were not events that would normally receive radio or television coverage. It certainly would be unlikely that a gardening club's installation luncheon would get the attention of the electronic media, for the audience would be too limited.

In the next chapter, you'll learn what does get the attention of radio and TV news editors and producers.

# CHAPTER 5

# GETTING TV AND RADIO COVERAGE

Although newspapers will sometimes cover the "ho-hum, pardon the yawn" events if things are slow, television and radio news departments will not. They need "quickies," attention-grabbers, imagination-sparkers. The time devoted to local news is just too incredibly short to give time to anything mundane.

Many of the same principles used in getting publicity in newspapers apply to television and radio as well. These forms of media also need to know the "who, what, when, where, and why" just as a newspaper does. They also need sufficient advance notice for proper scheduling.

As with print media, you should first determine whether you want only advance publicity, such as a listing on a station's "Community Calendar," or if you want to appear on a talk show, or maybe have a reporter and/or cameraman on hand, capturing your event on video for the eleven o'clock news.

The "Community Calendar" segments are spot announcements for upcoming events (usually for non-profit organizations) called Public Service Announcements (PSA's). Stations do these without charge as a service to their communities. A PSA is from ten to sixty seconds long and is read by the show's host, usually from an index card.

You have probably seen or heard such announcements in your area and know which local stations have such a service. If you do not know where to direct your public service announcement, check your public library for professional directories that list that kind of information, such as *Finder Binder, Bacon's Publicity Checker, and Broadcasting Cable Yearbook.*

Of course, if you are interested in getting something on your local station, you could call the station and ask the switchboard operator who is in charge of PSA's. The operators at TV and radio stations are amazing. Two days after they start the job, they know everyone and everything involved in running the station.

*Do not* call and ask for "the station manager." At best, you will get his secretary and will have to explain to her what you want. You will not get through to him, for she knows that (1) he does not have time for that, and (2) he does not handle that type of thing anyway. He's the executive who deals with corporate and department heads. So you'll save time and aggravation if you just ask the operator to direct you to the proper person.

Once you have determined the name of the person who handles PSA's, you are ready to compose your release. But rather than putting "FOR IMMEDIATE RELEASE" at the top, as you normally would for a regular news release, put the words "PUBLIC SERVICE ANNOUNCEMENT" at the top of the sheet, followed two spaces below by the date(s) your announcement should air.

Then write out exactly what you would like announced on the community calendar. Make sure you have included all the necessary information in a clear, concise, easy-to-read manner. By all means, include the name and telephone number of the contact person in case the station desires more information.

On the following page is a PSA for the Borrego Spring Grapefruit Festival, held each year in Borrego Springs, California. It is one example of how public service announcements are done.

The preceding PSA was mailed to radio and television stations throughout Southern California. Because of the mass mailing, it would have been impractical to determine the name of the person handling PSA's at each station. Therefore, publicity chairwoman Jean Peterson addressed it to: Public Service Director, "Community Calendar."

This is quite acceptable, and she had no problem with the PSA reaching the proper persons.

Peterson also sent a cover letter (often called a "pitch" letter in industry slang), which gave additional information on the festival. Sometimes this type of additional data prompts stations to do a follow-up story on an event. Her cover letter is shown on page 59.

Public service announcements are usually included on a first-come, first-served basis, just as

in newspapers' "Upcoming Events" sections; so be sure you get your PSA in their hands at least three weeks before your event is to occur.

Advance notice of about two to three weeks is also advisable if you want to see yourself on the evening news. It isn't that news assignment editors schedule their day books that far in advance necessarily; but if they think you or your event might make a good segment, it gives them enough time to squeeze in a call to you sometime in the interim to get any further information they may need, such as explicit directions on how to get to the location.

Also, when you check the media directories at the library, make sure you jot down the FAX number for the station. If you have heard nothing from them within three days of your scheduled event, send them a FAX. A FAX carries a sense of urgency that a letter or news release just can't match, and it may get their attention.

If you want to appear on a radio or television talk show, you should send your news release (and a photograph for TV) to the station approximately four weeks prior to the time you wish to appear. This is just a guideline, you understand, for guests are sometimes scheduled on much shorter notice.

It's a good idea to call the day prior to the scheduled date and confirm the arrangements with your contact person. This is as much for the station's benefit as for yours, for they like to know that you are still alive and well, that your flight has not been grounded because of bad weather, and that you are still planning to be there.

And by all means, whatever type of coverage you are seeking, *say* it in your cover letter, and make sure you address it to the right person. If you want to get on a talk show, for example, don't address your query to the host of the show. Find out the name of the producer; then send information or queries to that person.

If your news release captures the producer's interest because it would be of interest to viewers

CONTACT:  Jean Peterson, Publicity Chairman
(619) 767-5555;  Home: (619) 767-3412

March 1, 1991

Air:  March 1 through April 5

### PUBLIC SERVICE ANNOUNCEMENT

The annual BORREGO SPRING GRAPEFRUIT FESTIVAL will be held in Borrego Springs from April 6 through April 21.  For information, call: (619) 767-5555.

In addition to the FESTIVAL events, there will be a hidden TREASURE CHEST filled with free prizes for the finder.

-end-

622 Palm Canyon Dr., Borrego Springs, CA 92004 **MAILING ADDRESS**: P.O. Box 671, Borrego Springs, CA 92004
TELEPHONE (619) 767-5555 FAX (619) 767-5963  OFFICE HOURS - 10am-4pm, 7 Days, October thru May

March 1, 1991

Public Service Director
"Community Calendar"

Dear Producer:

The annual BORREGO SPRING GRAPEFRUIT FESTIVAL, April 6 through
April 21, is sponsored by the Borrego Springs Chamber of Commerce.
This non-profit event is designed to provide pleasure and recreation
for visitors of all ages.

The varied events scheduled during the three FESTIVAL weekends
appeal to a wide range of interests and a diverse population.  For
many visitors to the FESTIVAL, this is their first exposure to the
Anza-Borrego Desert State Park - the largest state park in the U.S.

By publicizing the GRAPEFRUIT FESTIVAL, we also promote one of the
most intriguing natural environments in America.

As you know, the small resort town of Borrego Springs is located
within the 600,000 acres of the Anza-Borrego Desert State Park.
Because of our location, we enjoy the unique opportunity to be an
integral part of all the Park has to offer.

In fact, some of the GRAPEFRUIT FESTIVAL events include those that
are strictly related to the Anza-Borrego Desert State Park. For
example:  slide show and lecture by a Park Ranger; guided desert
walks; seminar on the "Cultural Heritage of Anza-Borrego"; Indian
Dances; B.Y.O.B. (bring your own binoculars) Star Party; Anza-
Borrego Park Symposium.

We appreciate your help in letting the public know about the
BORREGO SPRING GRAPEFRUIT FESTIVAL.  If you have any questions,
please call me at your convenience.

Sincerely,


Jean Peterson, Publicity Chairman
(619) 767-5555, Chamber of Commerce; or
(619) 767-3412, home phone

622 Palm Canyon Dr., Borrego Springs, CA 92004 MAILING ADDRESS: P.O. Box 671, Borrego Springs, CA 92004
TELEPHONE (619) 767-5555 FAX (619) 767-5963  OFFICE HOURS - 10am-4pm, 7 Days, October thru May

or listeners, you are likely to get the coverage you seek.

Remember, these producers are busy people. They work at a pace that gives new meaning to the words "stress levels." So whatever you can do to make it easier for them, helps you.

For example, Dave Alexander, program director for KKHT-FM, Springfield, Missouri, says, "I get impatient when I have to wade through pages of type to find out what it is a person wants or what he or she has to offer."

Karen Carter, producer of the popular talk show, "Drive Time Radio," heard on KSDO-AM, in San Diego, California, says, "I like to see in bold letters across the top of a news release: *the subject*. For example, Police Brutality—so at a quick glance I know if it's on diets, taxes, war, etc."

According to Carter, an ideal talk show guest is colorful, knowledgeable, and articulate. If the guest's topic is timely (an expert on romance on Valentine's Day, or a spokesperson for a patriotic organization on the 4th of July, for example), the person has an even better chance of getting on the show.

The same general principles apply when you wish to have coverage on a TV news broadcast. Your subject has to be pertinent and timely and the arrangements must be made in advance.

However, if you have given a station plenty of lead time and it has agreed to send a reporter, don't get angry if no one shows up.

"Oh, yeah?" you say. "After I told everyone and his uncle that I was going to be on TV? After they promised, I shouldn't be angry?"

That's right. Disappointed, yes. Angry, no. I'll tell you why.

Television and radio are branches of the media in which "immediate" is the operative word. Those in charge may have thought you or your organization's event sounded very interesting when they heard about it three weeks ago. They may have still been planning to cover it three days ago or three hours ago. Then a four-alarm fire breaks out in the downtown business district, and the reporting team assigned to your story is rescheduled to cover the fire.

Sure it's disappointing, but getting angry won't help. You could call up the station and scream at your contact person until you are hoarse, but it won't change a thing. Plus, the next time you want publicity, no one will even make the effort.

All you can do is make the arrangements and pray that some inconsiderate criminal does not pick that particular time to rob a bank, take hostages, and hold the S.W.A.T. team at bay with a homemade hand grenade.

A bank robbery or a big fire both have news values (conflict and disaster, remember?). You or your organization's event may have news value, too. You may have talked the mayor into dressing up like a chicken and presenting the key to the city to your grand poopah. That would have prominence and it would certainly have novelty, but conflict and disaster are the news values that are going to take precedence. The saying goes, "If it bleeds, it leads."

But assuming that a big fire doesn't break out or that the criminals are laying low at the time, what kind of event is a television or radio station most likely to cover?

The following are a few events in our area that have been covered by radio or TV.

A radio station did a broadcast at a chili cook-off fundraiser for the Make-A-Wish Foundation. The event was held at an auto race track and there were lots of exhibits and games and bands playing. The station did a number of on-air interviews with contestants and members of the Make-A-Wish Foundation.

A local TV station sent a crew to cover a birthday party for a ninety-five-year old lady who had taken up bowling at eighty-five and had not missed a week since then. The party was given by the lady's bowling league and was, of course, held at the bowling alley, which also received good publicity.

This event had a lot of human interest value and it had a lot of action. (When they say, "Lights, camera, action," they want action.) Not only did they get a shot of the lady bowling, but a Groucho look-alike bounded onto the lanes to wish her well and hand her some balloons.

This event almost fell into the category of what one newscaster friend calls "the no kidding stories." You know the kind. A cat adopts a squirrel. Joe says to Sam, "I saw a cat nursing a squirrel on TV news last night."

Sam says, "No kidding?"

If you told your friend about a ninety-five-year old lady who hadn't missed a week's bowling in ten years, your friend might very likely reply, "No kidding?"

The "Ugly Dog Contest," sponsored by a shopping mall's merchants, got TV coverage. And a couple of fund-raising fashion shows in which TV personalities appeared as models got short spots. Events attended by visiting congressmen or senators usually get TV coverage because these events have the news values of eminence and prominence.

In attempting to persuade a television or radio station to give you coverage, first ask yourself, "Will this interest the viewers (listeners)?" Then ask yourself what news values are involved.

Remember, a station is not in business to give you publicity. It is in business to inform and/or entertain its audience. The news editor or producer must keep this in mind constantly. When they receive a news release, they don't say to themselves, "It would be nice to give this publicity." Instead they say, "Will our audience be interested in this?"

So, what is it about you, your product, your event or whatever you are trying to promote that is going to benefit, inform, or entertain that audience in some way? Stress that aspect in your news release.

In other words, if you want TV or radio coverage, what you have to offer must be newsworthy in order to get attention.

It may be difficult to get TV and/or radio coverage, but it is not impossible. After all, people do it all the time. However, a station must be selective, for time is limited. But, even at that, a station has to fill time for every single talk show or news broadcast.

What if a scheduled guest on a talk show does not show up? Could they call on you at the last minute? If so, are you articulate and entertaining? Can you give short, but informative answers to any questions asked about your subject?

You have never witnessed real panic until you have seen the news staff at a television station on a day when absolutely nothing is happening. You won't hear them saying, "No news is good news." Around a TV news department, no news is *not* good news.

At times like that, a station is very happy to cover anything that has news value. So, you may get lucky if your event occurs on a slow news day.

August, in non-election years, is usually a good time to get coverage from radio and television stations.

Why?

Because (1) there are no holidays in August; (2) many social and service clubs go "dark" during the summer and are not sponsoring events; and (3) school is out in many areas and a lot of people are on vacation; so things are usually slow.

But any time of the year is a good time if you can get the attention of the right person.

Let's take a look at some actual news releases that have received attention from radio and TV stations.

The release on pages 62 and 63 is one which prompted Karen Carter, KSDO-AM talk show producer, to schedule author Mary Donkersloot as

# News from Simon & Schuster

Simon and Schuster Building
1230 Avenue of the Americas
New York, New York 10020
Telephone:  212-698-7541

FOR IMMEDIATE RELEASE
Contact: Michele Farinet
212/698-7535

# THE FAST-FOOD DIET

## Quick and Healthy Eating at Home and on the Go

Every day millions of Americans take advantage of such fast foods as deli items, refrigerated convenience foods, frozen foods, and the foods from the quick-service restaurants that give rise to the term "fast food." Whether it's because there is no time for lunch or because the prospect of preparing dinner is too time-consuming, almost everyone at one time or another relies on foods that have already been prepared or can be prepared quickly.  As THE FAST-FOOD DIET: Quick and Healthy Eating at Home and on the Go (Simon & Schuster; April 18, 1991; $19.95) explains, it is easier than ever to eat fast and healthfully.

Author Mary Donkersloot, a registered dietitian, has devised a simple scoring system exclusive to THE FAST-FOOD DIET which rates all of the fast foods on a scale from 1 to 10. The higher the rating, the better the choice. The scale takes into account total fat, saturated fat, cholesterol, salt, sugar, fiber, vitamins, and minerals. The goal is to eat more top-rated foods (8, 9, or 10) and fewer low-rated ones (1-5). Here's how it works.

Wendy's ever-expanding SuperBar offers fast-food options in the form of baked potatoes, chili, fruit salads, and a hot and cold buffet. Donkersloot rates these potatoes and salads highest on her chart. Two slices of Domino's Veggie pizza (mushrooms, onions, green peppers, double cheese and olives) only rates a 6, but still beats a Hardee's steak biscuit which loses additional points due to high sugar content. Although Kentucky Fried Chicken's corn-on-the-cob is the best choice on their menu, it rates an 8. Jack-in-the-Box's Chicken Fajita Pita (including lettuce, tomatoes, onions and cheese) is still a better choice with a rating of 9. Burger King's

-more-

Whopper and french fries rates a 3 and 4 respectively. Donkersloot explains that all foods have some nutrients, but low-rated foods have too much fat and cholesterol. They need not be avoided completely, but a diet should have more high-rated foods than low-rated ones to be nutritionally sound.

Donkersloot has assigned a rating to popular dishes in over 17 fast-food restaurants and to boxed foods, canned goods and frozen meals, too. She includes chapters on breakfast, lunch, dinner, and snacks with helpful suggestions. "The basic fast-food breakfast should include a protein, a complex carbohydrate and a fruit. Balance is most important--too little protein may make you hungry, too much carbohydrates can make you sleepy." Each of these chapters conclude with charts of several ideal meals which score high and are quick and easy to prepare or order in a restaurant or take-out. Donkersloot's 21-day diet concentrates on "sensible, gradual, lasting weight loss," not only by a decrease of caloric intake but with a balance of calories as well. The plan outlined in THE FAST FOOD DIET will not only reduce fat intake but also "help you get optimal amounts of protein and complex carbohydrates, along with vitamins, minerals, and other micronutrients."

"Remember to eat sparingly at fast-food restaurants. Instead of the big--the Whopper, the Super, et cetera--choose the standard or the small. Supplement with a salad and low fat milk (in place of a shake) and you'll cut your fast-food calories in half and get twice the fiber, vitamins A and C, and calcium. You'll leave with a comfortable feeling too."

To make your fast-food regimen even easier, THE FAST FOOD DIET includes over 100 recipes for quick (under 20 minutes) meals to make at home. Tips on freezing fresh food, preparation, and general rules for time-saving cooking methods are also included.

THE FAST-FOOD DIET recipe section boasts many brown bag specialties, salads and salad dressings, soups, main dishes, party snacks, and desserts. Understanding many people's aversion to the idea of actually cooking, Donkersloot begins each of her recipes with the concept of "simplify."

THE FAST-FOOD DIET is just what people who are on the go have been waiting for--eating healthfully without modifying their active lifestyle. As Mary Donkersloot concludes: "This is your guide to living fast, eating well, and feeling better."

###

ABOUT THE AUTHOR:

Mary Donkersloot, R.D. is a personal nutritionist and founder of her own nutritional consulting firm, Personal Nutrition Management in San Diego, California. She is the media spokesperson in Southern California for the California Dietetic Association and has a weekly radio call-in program in San Diego.

a guest on "Drive Time Radio," hosted by Danuta. You can see why this release caught the producer's eye, because (1) the subject is clearly stated at the top of the sheet; (2) as a registered dietitian, Donkersloot has expertise in her subject; and (3) since most people are interested in their health, yet frequently eat on the run, the subject had great appeal to the listeners.

You'll recognize the newsworthiness of this next release, if you've ever had to explain sex to your children. Author Lynn Leight's book, *Raising Sexually Healthy Children*, covers a subject to which a wide audience can relate. Sharyn Rosenblum, senior publicist for Avon Books, reports that the news release resulted in author Lynn Leight being well received by radio and television in the four cities she visited on her media tour. In these cities she appeared as a guest on 18 talk shows.

You can see from the news release on pages 65 and 66 that there were news values galore to prompt producers to have Leight as a guest.

And do you think some people who have money problems could use a bit of sound advice on how to straighten out their financial mess? If so, after reading the next example, you will understand why articles on Jean Ross Peterson's book were published in many newspapers and magazines, such as *USA Today, The Los Angeles Times, Good Housekeeping*, and *Sylvia Porter's Personal Finance*, and why the producers of 163 radio and nine TV shows across the country asked her to be a guest.

Her flyer, which acted as a news release and prompted the invitations, is shown on page 67.

Laura Buxton, co-producer as well as co-host for KGTV's "Inside San Diego," says she likes to receive material that gets right to the point. "Like most TV producers, I constantly go at such a fast pace that I have the attention span of a gnat," she says. "So, I like to see the who, what, when, where, and why without a lot of 'hype' involved. Some

people, in attempting to make their subject seem more interesting, try to be cute and clever in their news releases. After you've been in this business a couple of years, you grow immune to all the sugar-coating. I'm interested in seeing a good story angle and some brief, but informative, backup material, such as a newspaper article on the person, which indicates he or she would make a good guest."

The letter on page 68 from Jennifer Nestegard, assistant manager of publicity and public relations for the Queen Mary and Spruce Goose, provided just the kind of straight-forward information Buxton likes to see. It prompted her to have Bill Winberg, historian for the Queen Mary, as a guest on "Inside San Diego."

Even though Nestegard sent the information in letter form, the first paragraph referring to the Queen Mary's darker side and paranormal activity is an ideal beginning and could easily have been the "hook" on a news release using the standard format.

The letter also clearly shows that Winberg, author of two books on the Queen Mary, has expertise in his subject.

The examples just shown were all on authors who had written books covering subjects that would interest a large segment of the viewing or listening audience. That does not mean you have to write a book before you will be able to get a spot on radio or TV. But it doesn't hurt, for it indicates that you have a thorough knowledge of your subject and a wealth of information which could be beneficial to the public.

Another reason authors show up so often on TV talk shows is because they (or their publishers) are willing to bear the expenses involved in traveling to distant cities to appear on television in order to promote a book. For, with few exceptions, talk show guests are not paid, nor are their hotel and travel expenses reimbursed by a TV station.

If you are on a limited budget and cannot afford to travel, you may have to limit your television appearances to your local stations.

# ◢ News from AVON BOOKS

105 Madison Avenue, New York, N.Y. 10016
Publicity Department: (212) 481-5640
Director of Publicity: Scott Manning

For Immediate Release
For More Information,
Contact: Sharyn Rosenblum
212/481-5639

EXPERT GUIDES PARENTS THROUGH "THE BIRDS AND THE BEES"

"Sexuality is all of who we are -- It is to be
enjoyed and celebrated."
--Lynn Leight, author of
RAISING SEXUALLY HEALTHY CHILDREN

In the nearly 60% of American households raising children, the issue of
sex education is a growing concern for many of today's parents. According to
Lynn Leight, Sexuality Counselor, Educator, Registered Nurse and Executive Director of a national network of Sex, Health, Education Centers, parents and
caregivers increasingly confess that they are too embarrassed and inhibited to
initiate a discussion with their children about sexual issues. These issues may
be related to nudity, pregnancy, menstruation, wet dreams, intercourse or the
emotional and physical changes associated with a child's emerging sexuality. In
her book RAISING SEXUALLY HEALTHY CHILDREN: A Loving Guide for Parents, Teachers, and Care-Givers (Avon Books, May 1990, $8.95 US/$10.95 Canada), Leight
provides parents with the accurate information, strategies and guidelines necessary to give children healthy sexual attitudes, self-esteem, and self-worth.

Leight clearly illustrates how a child begins learning about sexuality at
birth, and, for better or worse, parents are the primary instructors. She
reveals how parents who avoid discussing sexuality with their child, or deny
their child's sexual curiosities, are effectively abandoning his/her sex education to the media, inaccurate peers, and our sex-saturated culture. Open sexual
dialogue between parent and child, however, can enable the child to understand
and cope with the many myths and negative sexual messages portrayed through
pornography, advertising, music and television. Exposure to such exploitative
and confusing images, without a proper perspective, may negatively color a
child's sense of responsibility and self-worth which in turn can possibly lead
to sexual dysfunction in adulthood.

-MORE-

"A child needs more than a one-time sexuality lesson about 'the birds and the bees' to become comfortable with his/her sexuality," says Leight. She encourages parents to take advantage of ordinary everyday encounters and turn them into spontaneous sexuality learning experiences. There are dozens of "Golden Opportunities," as she calls them, when a parent can initiate relaxed, open talks at every age and every stage of maturation.

In RAISING SEXUALLY HEALTHY CHILDREN, Leight helps parents to better understand their own sexuality by developing an openness with their child. She shows how guiding a child through the sexual developmental stages may enable a parent to reconcile his/her own feelings of negative self-worth. Moreover, they can overcome sexual fears which may have resulted from inadequate sexual education.

Teaching a child about sex is a greater challenge today than ever before. "Looking ahead to the increasing danger of AIDS and new strains of sexually transmitted diseases, we see the time has come to legitimize a child's right to know," asserts Leight. "Honest communication about sexuality is necessary to preserve the health, welfare, and personal happiness of your child."


About the Author

Lynn Leight, a certified sexuality counselor, educator and registered nurse, is founder and executive director of seventeen Sex, Health, Education (S.H.E.) centers nationwide. She has counseled thousands of children and their parents and leads national and international seminars for adults, teens, teachers, nurses, and other health professionals. She regularly appears on local and national TV and radio shows to share her innovative ideas. She is adjunct assistant professor at the University of Miami School of Family Medicine, adjunct professor at the University of Miami School of Nursing, and a doctoral candidate at the Institute for the Advanced Study of Human Sexuality. She is married for 33 years, has three children and lives with her family in North Miami, Florida.

RAISING SEXUALLY HEALTHY CHILDREN
Avon Books
May 1990
$8.95 US/$10.95 Canada

###

# HAVE YOU EVER SAID? . . . **MY FINANCES ARE A MESS!!**

*Do you want to . . .*

- always know every fact and figure about your finances?
- find a fast and easy way to keep lifetime records?
- have peace of mind about your financial future?
- spend only 20 minutes a week at your desk?
- increase your capital and investments?
- be your own expert money manager?

*Editors of* Sylvia Porter's Personal Finance *declare Peterson "one of the best-organized financial authorities we know."*

Sex, age, education, occupation—there are no requirements for success. "Personal financial freedom is a reality for everyone," says Jean Ross Peterson, author of TURN CHAOS INTO CASH: A Complete Guide to Organizing and Managing Your Personal Finances.

Peterson gives you the same effective plan she teaches in her lectures and to her clients. Now you can take control of your finances and increase your wealth.

- Can record keeping actually earn you extra money?
- Why is an ATM hazardous to your financial health?
- Who is your "financial buddy"?
- Where and how can you find some "free" money?
- How can you control impulse spending?
- Are credit cards your friend or your enemy?
- Are there errors in your social security records?
- Is a budget a waste of time and effort? (Yes!)
- Which records should you keep—and how long should you keep them?

TURN CHAOS INTO CASH answers these questions . . . and many more. Plus it includes the bonus Lifetime Financial Workbook to guarantee your success as an expert money manager.

Peterson, a graduate of Stanford University and a specialist in economic education, is regularly quoted in national publications on topics related to family and personal finances. Some examples are: *USA TODAY, Los Angeles Times, US Air, Good Housekeeping,* and *Sylvia Porter's Personal Finance.* The author is a frequent guest on radio and TV. Among her popular books is the highly regarded IT DOESN'T GROW ON TREES.

**TURN CHAOS INTO CASH** is available in bookstores and from the publisher.

**Jean Ross Peterson**

Please send me____copy/copies of TURN CHAOS INTO CASH ($8.95). Virginia residents add 4% sales tax. Include $1.50 for postage and handling.

(Please print) NAME_____

ADDRESS_____

CITY_____STATE_____ZIP_____

(No cash or C.O.D.'s) Mail to: Betterway Publications, Box 219, Crozet, Virginia 22932. (804) 823-5661.

QUEEN MARY & SPRUCE GOOSE®

April 12, 1991

Laura Buxton
McGraw-Hill
Inside San Diego
P.O. Box 85347
San Diego, CA 92138

Dear Ms. Buxton:

For years the famed luxury liner, the Queen Mary, has been known for her elegance and splendor. But have you heard the Queen Mary has a darker side? The Queen Mary has also been the site of hundreds of reports of paranormal activity. Most of these unexplained incidents have occurred in areas off limits to the public. This year, the Queen Mary & Spruce Goose Entertainment Center is conducting tours in these areas to explain the haunting past of the great luxury liner.

In conjunction with the latest chapter in the Queen Mary's history, we would like you to consider the Queen Mary's historian, Mr. Bill Winberg, as an interview subject for your show. Mr. Winberg has been a crewmember on the Queen Mary for over 11 years, six of which have dealt specifically with archival material and preservation. Mr. Winberg is also the co-author of the books A Visit to the Queen Mary & Spruce Goose (1985) and The Queen Mary Pictorial (1986) Mr. Winberg would be able to provide your show with historic footage of the ocean liner dating back to her legendary heyday as well as current footage in which members of the ship's crew reveal their encounters with the reported ghosts on board.

Knowing you book guests well in advance, I realize there may not be an available opening at the present time. However, I will be contacting you this week to determine if there is any interest in future bookings. If you would like to reach me prior to that time, please call at (213) 435-3511, Ext. 1248.

Sincerely,

Jennifer Nestegard
Assistant Manager
Publicity & Public Relations

Hotel Queen Mary • Queen Mary & Spruce Goose Attractions • Londontowne
Pier J • Post Office Box 8 • Long Beach, California 90801
Telephone (213) 435-3511

However, do not let lack of travel funds deter you from sending news releases to radio stations in distant cities, for they will often conduct interviews by telephone. The sound quality is so good these days that it seems as if the guest is right in the studio with the talk show host or newscaster, when, in fact, the guest may be thousands of miles away.

Just to reassure you, many people get on radio and television without having written a book. In the following chapters, you will see more examples of news releases that led to coverage by the electronic media as well as by newspapers and magazines.

# CHAPTER 6

# NEWS RELEASES FOR BUSINESS

Previously, we touched briefly on how news releases can help increase your business and/or profits. If you are a business person trying to learn how to promote your own product or service through writing effective news releases, this section of the book will probably interest you the most. But if your busy schedule has prompted you to skip a few chapters and turn directly to this page, you will have missed some important basics discussed in earlier chapters.

If you've been diligent in studying the first few chapters, you are probably getting a good idea by now of what makes a news release effective. However, you may wonder whether or not news releases for businesses differ from other news releases.

The answer is: a news release for a business is basically the same as any good news release.

However, according to 111 business and financial editors from thirty-six states who responded to a survey by Brouillard Communications, business releases are often poorly written and lacking in local significance.

Other reasons these editors gave for tossing the news releases into the wastebasket were: (1) an appropriate contact person was not listed or was impossible to reach by telephone; (2) the release was too "wordy," boring, or filled with "puff;" (3) it lacked reader appeal; and (4) it was not received in time.

Therefore, just as in any news release, a release for a business must show from whom it came, the name and telephone number of an available contact person, and contain complete information (the Five W's) in the body.

In a news release for a business, it is especially important to have an attention-grabbing headline and a "hook" for the opening in order to make what you have to "sell" as interesting and newsworthy as possible.

The reason is quite simple. Newspapers are not prone to publicizing businesses that might otherwise buy advertising, since advertising revenues are what keep them in business. Yet, an editor is always on the lookout for stories that will be of interest to readers. Therefore, getting news values into a news release for a business is of utmost importance if you want to get an editor's attention.

A news release from the New York-based magazine *Business Tokyo* (pages 72-74), which included excellent backup data, is one that captured the interest of Cheryl Hall, business editor of *The Dallas Morning News*.

Although Japan is far from Texas, this news release still contained the news value of *proximity* for readers in Dallas because of Japanese investments in the area. The question of Japanese investments in the United States was also being discussed in Congress at the time and was being addressed on many radio and TV news programs and talk shows across the country. Hall could see that the subject was *timely*. She also knew that the specifics of which Japanese companies were investing the most and which countries were receiving the heaviest investments would be of interest to the readers.

This news release generated the story shown on page 75 which was published in *The Dallas Morning News*.

Because the *Business Tokyo* news release gave lots of interesting facts and figures, it also resulted in stories in a number of other newspapers, including *USA Today* and the *Mainichi Daily News*, an English-language daily paper published in Japan. Since *Business Tokyo* was mentioned as an intrinsic part of the story, it also generated a good deal of publicity for the magazine itself.

Wise entrepreneurs recognize the significance of having their businesses mentioned in print, even if obliquely—a significance that small business owners sometimes do not grasp.

For example, a few years ago a friend of mine relocated in this area and set about trying to establish his good name as a house painter. I pointed out that the local historical society's building needed painting and suggested he offer to furnish his labor for free if the historical society would furnish the paint. I told him it would give him an opportunity to make new friends, and the building would serve as an example of the quality

of his work. I also pointed out that a "face lift" on the beloved building would probably receive newspaper coverage in which his name would be mentioned.

"I'm not giving away a week's worth of work free," he said. And that was the end of that.

However, I know, from the following example, that this kind of community service not only can benefit others but can be rewarding for the donor as well.

In the small town of Idyllwild, California, there grew a large tree for which the townspeople

---

**WHY NEWS RELEASES
ARE REJECTED**

Numerous studies have been done on why news releases are trashed. In one study conducted some years ago by the Lock Haven Express, Lock Haven, Pennsylvania, all of the rejected news releases were saved for two weeks. At the end of this time a total of 383 rejected releases from 182 sources were analyzed. The following reasons were given for discarding them:

1. No local angle
2. Lack of timeliness
3. Poor news writing
4. Too long
5. Too commercial
6. Sneaking company names into seemingly inconspicquos places
7. Gearing releases to influence editors more than to provide material for news columns

Similar studies by others have shown almost identical reasons for rejecting news releases.

FOR IMMEDIATE RELEASE
April 15, 1991
CONTACT:
Marc Perton,
212-633-1880

BUSINESS TOKYO

104 FIFTH AVENUE

NEW YORK, NY 10011

TEL / 212-633-1880

FAX / 212-633-2381

### *BUSINESS TOKYO* Publishes the *BT 100*:
### The Definitive List of Japanese Investors in America

Since 1985, Japanese investors have spent billions of dollars investing in and acquiring U.S. companies. With the buyouts of firms ranging from CBS Records to Talbots to Thermos, there is hardly an industry in America untouched by Japanese money. And while Japanese companies continue to invest in Europe and Asia, most of the money is still coming to the United States. These are just some of the facts revealed in the **BT 100**, the first definitive study of Japanese direct investment in the United States, which appears in the May issue of *Business Tokyo*. The magazine plans to update the list annually, making it the standard reference for information about Japanese direct investment in America.

Capped by Matsushita Electric Industrial, which acquired MCA for $6.1 billion, the **BT 100** list is the first of its kind. It ranks the top 100 Japanese investors in America from 1985 to 1990 and includes their total number of deals and target investments. "Japanese investment in the United States kicked into high gear in 1985," the magazine points out. "The economy was booming, the value of the yen shot up from 250 to 135 yen to the dollar and capital was still cheap — if cash-heavy Japanese companies needed to raise any."

In addition to the main list of Japanese investors, the **BT 100** features an in-depth analysis of Japanese investment patterns, with detailed charts showing which industries, regions and companies have received the most Japanese interest. The entertainment industry tops the list in dollar terms, with over $12 billion, while the computer industry received the most interest in terms of numbers of deals. California was the most active state for Japanese investment in 1990, with over 60 deals. The magazine also analyzes changing trends in Japanese investment. While the number of Japanese investments in U.S. firms has gone up, for example, the dollar value for each deal has dropped. In 1990, the median deal was $8.5 million, down from $23 million in 1988. Japanese companies are becoming more savvy about their investments, *Business Tokyo* points out. "A year ago, investment bankers were setting the parameters," says John A. Herrmann, president and CEO of the Bridgeford Group, the Industrial Bank of Japan's M&A arm. "The deals in today's market are being done Japanese-style rather than American style."

Japanese influence on American industry, according to the *Business Tokyo* article, cannot be ignored. Japanese control one quarter of the U.S. car market and have a virtual lock on consumer electronics. "Is there anything we look at more than our television sets or cars?" asks Martin K. Starr, a Columbia University Business School expert on cross-border investment.

The sharp increase in Japanese investment in the U.S. has led to fear, anger and frustration among many Americans. A recent Japan Society survey found that 75% of Americans think "Japanese are gaining too much control over the U.S. economy," and government responses have ranged from the Exon-Florio amendment, which allows the government to review foreign business deals for national-security implications, to calls for new tax reporting requirements for U.S. subsidiaries of foreign firms.

Despite such difficulties, Japanese investment in the United States will continue to grow, *Business Tokyo* states. "As they become more firmly entrenched in America, Japanese firms may start to act more like the typical American company next door, acquiring the sensitivity needed to avoid lawsuits and, like other foreign multinationals, allowing American managers to control their piece of the pie. But whether with arms outstretched or folded firmly in defiance, more Americans will have to get used to working with the Japanese," the magazine concludes. "The **BT 100** will be around for some time to come."

FOR IMMEDIATE RELEASE
April 15, 1991
CONTACT:
Marc Perton,
212-633-1880

## *BT 100:* THE TOP 10
Japanese Direct Investors in America, 1985-1990
($ millions)

| COMPANY | VALUE OF ALL DISCLOSED DEALS | NOTABLE INVESTMENTS | AMOUNT OF DEAL |
|---|---|---|---|
| 1 Matsushita Electric Industrial | 6,124.8 | MCA | 6,124.8 |
| 2 Sony | 5,810.0 | CBS Records Columbia Pictures | 2,000.0 3,400.0 |
| 3 Bridgestone | 2,600.0 | Firestone Tire & Rubber | 2,600.0 |
| 4 Saison Group | 2,150.0 | Intercontinental Hotels | 2,150.0 |
| 5 Aoki Corp. | 1,530.0 | Westin Hotels & Resorts | 1,530.0 |
| 6 Dai-Ichi Kangyo Bank | 1,450.0 | CIT Group | 1,280.0 |
| 7 Dainippon Ink & Chemicals | 1,317.9 | Reichhold Chemicals | 600.0 |
| 8 Mitsubishi Corp. | 1,189.4 | Aristech Chemical | 872.6 |
| 9 Nippon Mining | 1,119.0 | Gould | 1,100.0 |
| 10 Nippon Life Insurance | 1,033.3 | Shearson Lehman (1) | 508.3 |

---

(1) Acquired only minority equity interest in the company.

For more information or a complete copy of the BT 100, contact Marc Perton,
Business Tokyo, 212-633-1880.

*Backup material sent with the news release on the preceding page included the chart above and the data on the following page.*

## Selected Data from the BT 100:
The Definitive List of Japanese Direct
Investors in America

### Geography of Direct Investment
**The most active states in 1990**

WASHINGTON (8 deals)

MASSACHUSETTS (12 deals)

NEW YORK (12 deals)

CALIFORNIA (61 deals)

PENNSYLVANIA (10 deals)

CONNECTICUT (9 deals)

HAWAII (5 deals)

Source: Japan M&A Reporter

## JAPAN'S FOREIGN DIRECT INVESTMENT

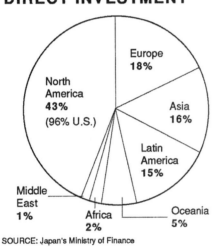

Europe 18%

North America 43% (96% U.S.)

Asia 16%

Latin America 15%

Middle East 1%

Africa 2%

Oceania 5%

SOURCE: Japan's Ministry of Finance

### Smaller Deals — but More of Them

Under $10 million

$10-$20 million

$20-$50 million

$50-$100 million

$100-$500 million

Over $500 million

The number of disclosed
transactions, by size of investment

1985 1986 1987 1988 1989 1990

Source: Japan M&A Reporter

## Cumulative Foreign Direct Investment in the United States*

| FDI as of 1989 ($billions) | | % growth over 1988 totals |
|---|---|---|
| 1 United Kingdom | $119.1 billion | 16.9% |
| 2 Japan | $69.7 billion | 30.6% |
| 3 Netherlands | $60.5 billion | 23.5% |
| 4 Canada | $31.5 billion | 15.3% |

*Includes greenfield investment

Source: Department of Commerce

CONTACT:
Marc Perton
Business Tokyo
104 Fifth Avenue
New York, NY 10011
212-633-1880

# Matsushita leads list of Japanese investors in U.S.

### By Richard Alm
*Staff Writer of* The Dallas Morning News

Despite paying $430 million to rescue Dallas' financially troubled Southland Corp., retailer Ito-Yokado Ltd. ranks only No. 17 among Japanese investors in the United States.

So says *Business Tokyo*, a glossy English-language magazine from Japan. On Monday, the publication released its first — by its reckoning, the world's first — top 100 list of Japanese companies that have bought chunks of Americana.

At the top of the ranking, Matsushita Electrical Industrial Co., with last year's megadeal for entertainment conglomerate MCA Inc., worth $6.1 billion. Sony Corp. comes in second at $5.8 billion after gobbling up CBS Records in 1987 and Columbia Pictures in 1989.

"This is the first time we've done a top 100 list," said Marc Perton at *Business Tokyo*'s New York office, "and as far as we can tell, no one else has ever done it. Frankly, it's about time. There's so much talk about Japanese investment in the United States."

The deal for Southland, a company deep in debt to junk bondholders until Ito-Yokado, the parent of 7-

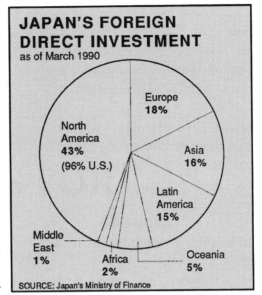

**JAPAN'S FOREIGN DIRECT INVESTMENT**
as of March 1990

North America 43% (96% U.S.)
Europe 18%
Asia 16%
Latin America 15%
Middle East 1%
Africa 2%
Oceania 5%

SOURCE: Japan's Ministry of Finance

*The Dallas Morning News*

Eleven Japan Co., bought a 70 percent stake, stood out in 1990, finishing third behind the MCA buyout and Mitsubishi Corp.'s $872 million purchase of Aristech Chemical Corp.

The *Business Tokyo* list tallies acquisitions of at least 50 percent of a company, purchases of divisions, investments of less than 50 percent and buyouts of joint ventures. It doesn't include "greenfield investments," where a company comes to the

Please see MATSUSHITA on Page 4D.

# Matsushita Japan's top U.S. investor

Continued from Page 1D.

United States and starts from scratch with its own subsidiary.

Japanese merger and acquisition activity didn't start its takeoff until 1985, when the declining value of the dollar made U.S. property suddenly cheaper to Japanese buyers. Japan's investment has swelled to a total of $70 billion, as of 1989, making Japan second only Britain, with $119 billion, as a foreign owner in America.

"There's hardly an industry in America untouched by Japanese money," Mr. Perton says.

As investment grew, Japanese purchases of U.S. properties became a lightning rod for critics of Japan, a nation whose economic success has made many Americans jittery. A Japan Society survey found that 75 percent of Americans agree that the "Japanese are gaining too much control over the U.S. economy."

The *Business Tokyo* survey spotted some trends:

■ The entertainment industry tops the list in dollar terms, with more than $12 billion. Finance ranks with $8.9 billion, followed by hotels and restaurants ($3.8 billion), automotive ($3.8 billion), health ($3.1 billion) and computers ($3 billion).

■ The computer industry had the most deals at 127. Finance came in second at 81, health third at 59.

## BUSINESS TOKYO VIEWS JAPAN'S U.S. BUYING SPREE

| Company | Total value (disclosed deals) | Big deals | Industry |
|---|---|---|---|
| 1. Matsushita Electrical Industrial | $6.124 billion | MCA | Entertainment |
| 2. Sony | $5.810 billion | CBS Records, Columbia Pictures | Entertainment |
| 3. Bridgestone | $2.600 billion | Firestone Tire & Rubber | Tires |
| 4. Saison Group | $2.150 billion | Intercontinental Hotels | Hotels |
| 5. Aoki Corp. | $1.530 billion | Westin Hotels & Resorts | Hotels and resorts |
| 6. Dai-Ichi Kangyo Bank | $1.450 billion | CIT Group | Asset-based lending |
| 7. Dainippon Ink & Chemicals | $1.317 billion | Reichhold Chemicals | Specialty chemicals |
| 8. Mitsubishi Corp. | $1.189 billion | Aristech Chemical | Chemicals and plastics |
| 9. Nippon Mining | $1.119 billion | Gould | Electronics |
| 10. Nippon Life Insurance | $1.033 billion | Shearson Lehman* | Brokerage |

*Minority interest
SOURCE: Business Tokyo

*The Dallas Morning News*

had great affection. They liked the tree so much that when the road was built, they paved around it and left it standing tall and proud in the middle of the street. But a few years ago, the tree sickened and died.

Meetings were held to decide what to do about the tree. Of course, the most obvious thing was to cut the tree down. But then a young artist named Jonathan LaBenne said, "No, we can't just cut it down. I'll carve it into a totem pole."

Which is exactly what LaBenne did—strictly out of a desire to help his community, for he did not charge a cent.

Idyllwild has just over 2,000 residents, but thousands of people flock into this Alpine-like community on weekends and vacations. When these thousands of people saw LaBenne perched forty feet or so up the tree, carving with a nine-pound chainsaw, word began to spread. Soon he and his project were being mentioned on radio and television, and stories about him and the totem pole appeared in newspapers and magazines.

"The rest," as they say, "is history." Those of you who have visited Yellowstone National Park since 1989 probably saw his ten-foot sculpture of a grizzly in the Old Faithful lodge. And people in Eastern Washington know of his work on the sixty-five foot Codger Pole—the largest chainsaw sculpture in the world—commemorating The Codger Bowl. LaBenne's work now sells for approximately $200 per foot, and he has so many orders it will take two years to complete them all.

Who knows where my house painter friend might be today had he been as generous of spirit as LaBenne? If he had opted to paint the historical society building, he could have sent out a news release on the project, such as the one on page 77.

If the historical society had paid a painting contractor to repaint the building, a newspaper probably would not mention the name of the business. But since Bill Jones donated his time,

he would undoubtedly be mentioned. Anyone who read the article and needed his house painted could see whether or not Bill Jones was a good painter by checking the Fremont Hotel. If Jones' prices were reasonable, he would very likely get a number of jobs as a result of the publicity.

Businesses which sell products can also benefit from charitable gifts. If you give one of your products to a worthy cause, let the world know about it through a news release. This is a simple way to get your business or name publicized.

Success in business doesn't depend so much on what kind of business you operate, but on how you operate the business. The majority of businesses fall someplace between the multi-million dollar corporations and a one-man house painting operation. But whatever your business, you have competition. Publicity about your business often helps to beat out the competition and can be the determining factor in whether you succeed or fail.

For example, although there are many dating services around the country, a goodly number have a short life span. Few are publicized in half-page feature articles on the front page of the "Lifestyles" section of a newspaper with over 100,000 circulation. But the news release on page 78 resulted in just that for a video dating service called Great Expectations.

This example demonstrates how news values were incorporated most effectively. The news release was sent prior to Valentine's Day (news value of *timeliness*) and the emphasis was not on dating, which would have limited reader interest, but on the art of flirting, something intriguing to many of us (news values of *novelty* and *sex* and *romance*).

The sample questions, such as, "What signals will attract a serious mate, not just a sexual partner?," and "What are the dangers of flirting incorrectly?," include news values of *progress or disaster* and *consequence*.

### JONES' HOUSE PAINTING
### 988 Manor Drive
### Bergtown, CA 90001

FOR IMMEDIATE RELEASE                     CONTACT: Bill Jones
                                          TELEPHONE: 555-9211
August 2, 2005

BERGTOWN HISTORICAL SOCIETY BUILDING TO GET FACE LIFT

Work will begin on Monday, August 5, on a face lift for the old
Fremont Hotel, headquarters of the Bergtown Historical Society.
The exterior will be repainted in time for the annual Pioneer Days
celebration to be held at the Fremont Hotel on August 24.

Labor for the mammoth painting job is being donated by Bill Jones
of Jones' House Painting.  Jones says, "I haven't lived in
Bergtown very long, but I've grown to love the area and appreciate
the people.  The Fremont is a fine old building, and a couple of
coats of paint will make it look good as new.  I felt this was
something I could do to show my appreciation for the kindness I've
been shown since I arrived."

For reservations to the Pioneer Days celebration, call Hattie Snow
of the Bergtown Historical Society at 555-6677.

###

**PUBLICITY INTERNATIONAL AGENCY**

*R.J. Garis—Publicist*                                    *(619) 467-1194 (CA)*

INTERVIEW ALERT

### FLIRTING FOR ROMANCE, FUN AND PROFIT!

EVERYONE HAS FLIRTED, EACH SEEKS A DIFFERENT RESULT. SOME WANT ROMANCE, WHILE OTHERS ARE HOPING TO GAIN ADVANTAGES IN BUSINESS OR CAREER. FLIRTING DONE RIGHT, CAN BE A POWERFUL TOOL.

VICTORIA PARKER IS PRESIDENT OF THE GREAT EXPECTATIONS FRANCHISE OWNERS ASSOCIATION (THE NATIONS LARGEST VIDEO DATING CHAIN). OVER THE YEARS, MS. PARKER HAS INTERVIEWED AND OBSERVED THOUSANDS OF MEN AND WOMEN ON FLIRTING. SHE HAS STUDIED THE TECHNIQUE'S THAT WORK AND THOSE THAT FAIL. MS. PARKER SAYS "ANYONE CAN LEARN TO SEND THE RIGHT SIGNALS AND ACHIEVE THE DESIRED RESULTS".

### SAMPLE QUESTIONS:

* WHAT SIGNALS WILL ATTRACT A SERIOUS MATE, NOT JUST A SEXUAL PARTNER?
* WHAT ARE THE DANGERS OF FLIRTING INCORRECTLY?
* DO MALES REACT DIFFERENTLY TO FLIRTING THAN FEMALES?
* IS THERE A SAFE WAY TO FLIRT FOR CAREER ENHANCEMENT?
* HOW SHOULD I REACT WHEN FLIRTED WITH BY SOMEONE ELSE?

**BACKGROUND:** VICTORIA PARKER HAS MADE A CAREER OUT OF HELPING PEOPLE ESTABLISH THE RELATIONSHIPS THEY DESIRE. SHE OWNS THREE COMPANIES DEDICATED TO HELPING PEOPLE MEET EACH OTHER. HER TECHNIQUES HAVE BROUGHT HER ENORMOUS PERSONAL AND ECONOMIC SUCCESS. IN JUST SEVEN YEARS MS. PARKER HAS GONE FROM BEING A WAITRESS TO A CURRENT WORTH OF MORE THAN $3 MILLION!

**AVAILABILITY:** VICTORIA PARKER IS BASED IN SAN DIEGO. SHE TRAVELS TO MANY CITIES AS A PROFESSIONAL SPEAKER AND MEDIA GUEST. TELEVISION, RADIO OR PRINT INTERVIEWS ARE INVITED. TELEPHONE INTERVIEWS MAY ALSO BE ARRANGED.

**CONTACT:** PUBLICIST R.J. GARIS - PUBLICITY INTERNATIONAL AGENCY (619) 467-1194 (CA)

*10464 Clairemont Mesa Blvd., Suite 118 • San Diego, California 92124*

# EQUAL OPPORTUNITY FLIRTING

**By Nancy Weingartner**
*Californian Staff writer*

Remember when men could get away with pickup lines such as "What's your sign?" and "Is your mother home?"

Women in the olden days may have fallen for such inept attempts at flirting, but today's woman requires a little more imagination, not to mention subtlety, if a man wants to gain her favors.

Women may not receive equal pay for equal work. They may still be doing more than their fair share of the household chores, but at least they no longer have to wait for a man to flirt with them.

Flirting is an equal opportunity activity.

It's also an art, according to Victoria Parker, owner of Great Expectations video dating service in San Diego.

And like any art, there are a few basic rules that have to be followed.

First of all, one of the 10 commandments of flirting is: Thou shall not flirt with a married person.

Unless, of course, you're married to that person and then it's not only acceptable, it's necessary.

Flirting is one way to keep the magic alive in a relationship, so you won't need her services, Parker said.

If you don't have a live-in partner to flirt with, Parker has some guidelines to maximize your flirting attempts.

Say you're waiting for the elevator and a likely target stands next to you. Before launching into a full-blown flirt, ask yourself what you hope to accomplish:

A) Do you want it to lead to a date?

B) Are you bored and looking for a diversion?

C) Are you in a playful mood and want to make someone's day?

D) Do you want to bear his children?

Once your motive is established, it's time to come up with some original lines.

"Don't ask a silly question," she warns. "It's better to make a statement."

One of Parker's favorite lines is:

"I like your gray-and-black combination. Did you dress yourself or did a lady help you?"

The beauty of this line is that it not only tells you whether he's attached or not, it can be adapted to any color scheme.

Men will have to come up with their own version of this particular line since most men don't dress women, unless they're fashion designers.

Be original.

Stay away from the weather as a topic of conversation—it's vastly overrated and, in Southern California, it's redundant.

A tip for men: women love to be treated like they have brains, so asking their opinion on the world situation is a good move. Just keep it lighthearted, no heavy stuff that can be depressing.

Humor is always appropriate.

The idea is to be spontaneous, Parker said. Say or do something that's not expected.

For instance, if you see someone in a restaurant you'd like to meet, Parker suggests sending flowers to the table instead of the more customary drink.

Passing messages via the waiter is another trick. If you're dining in a Chinese restaurant,

you might want to deliver your phone number inside a fortune cookie.

Flirting in a bar is not recommended because alcohol tends to put everyone at a disadvantage.

Flirt with your eyes, but don't give a come-hither look. It's too obvious and definitely passe, she said.

"Use eye contact, backed with a mental plan," she suggests.

"If you only get one shot, be proud of it" is another one of Parker's truisms.

To illustrate her point, Parker tells the story about the time she was at the Playboy mansion and James Caan walked in.

"I knew I had one shot so I tapped him on the shoulder and said, 'Do you know how I recognized you? (pause) It was your shoulders. Your incredibly square shoulders.' And then I left," she said.

She may not have become Mrs. James Caan, but she did make an impression on him and she was dating Barbie Benton's brother anyway so it didn't really matter.

The point is it was fun. It was flirting in the big leagues.

For those of us whose flirting will be limited to spouses, Parker advises people never to become predictable.

If you always wear sweats on the weekends, try dressing up some Sunday when you don't have plans to go out.

If you always whine about not cooking on Friday evenings, try cooking a gourmet meal some Friday — or whine about not cooking on a Thursday. If you only bring home flowers on Valentine's Day, shame on you. Try surprising her, or him, with a gift when it's not a national holiday. Keep him or her guessing. (nrw)

---

This particular "Interview Alert" acted as a "teaser." Packed with news values, it prompted Nancy Weingartner of *The Daily Californian* to call for a telephone interview to get a more complete story. She then wrote the feature article above, which was published on Valentine's Day.

In addition to receiving newspaper coverage, Victoria Parker, president of Great Expectations, also appeared on TV shows, such as KGTV's

"Inside San Diego," CBS News, and ABC News, and on twenty-six radio talk shows after this news release was sent to the media. As a result of the publicity, a great many new members joined Great Expectations, accounting for around $25,000 in sales.

This example also proves that an article about your business does not have to appear in the business section of a newspaper to get good results.

In fact, people who are interested in learning more about flirting probably read the Lifestyle section more often than the business section. (Not that businessmen/women never flirt, you understand. It has been known to happen.)

Often the best section of a newspaper in which your business can be publicized depends on the business. For example, University of Wisconsin professor Dr. Stuart Robertshaw's "business" is doing research on humor. But, in order to do research, he needed research subjects. How was he to get volunteers?

"Dr. Humor," as he is called, is very serious about the importance of humor. He wanted to draw attention to the value of humor, for he knew that without humor life is more difficult. (Anyone who has ever tried to shove into a line in front of someone without laugh lines can attest to that!)

So he founded the National Association for the Humor Impaired. He then wrote his first news release and sent it to newspapers, but not to their business sections. (Not that businessmen/women do not have senses of humor. That, too, has been known to happen.)

On page 81 is his news release. The content of this release was so irresistible that editors were interested. Notice the great opening "hooker" on his news release. In his first sentence, he has told the media what the subject is about and established his expertise.

This news release generated at least 105 newspaper articles nationwide.

Within eight months of sending out his news release, "Dr. Humor" had been a guest on ninety-seven radio talk shows, including shows on WLS radio in Chicago, KABC in Los Angeles, and stations in Canada and Australia; and had been approached about future appearances on the Phil Donahue, the Oprah Winfrey, and the David Letterman television shows. The publicity brought in more than 900 new members to the National Association for the Humor Impaired within a

year's time. At last count, it was still growing. Dr. Robertshaw is now on the national speaker's circuit. And it all started with one effective news release.

But if your business is decorating ostrich eggs, how would any of this apply to you?

It does not matter what your business is—decorating ostrich eggs, making quilts, typing manuscripts, running a small dress shop, operating a restaurant or shoe repair shop—publicity will help you succeed.

If yours is a small home-based business, your marketing aims and opportunities are the same as those of big corporations.

Take decorating ostrich eggs, for example. Can you answer the first question, "How would my product benefit the public?"

Well, wouldn't one of your beautifully decorated, elaborately designed eggs be a collector's item—something a child would treasure and an adult would display with pride? And aren't your eggs so unique that *novelty* would be a news value you could use in your news release?

How did you learn to make them? Did you while away your time when you were snowbound each winter on your grandparents' farm in northern Minnesota by watching your Swedish grandmother decorate eggs until you learned the art? If so, you can add *human interest* to your news release.

Is there a hot news story to which you can tie your news release? For instance, is the fabulous Faberge egg collection from Russia being displayed in your city or someplace nearby? That would add *timeliness* to your news release. Or perhaps the directory *Chase's Annual Events* lists a "National Week" of some sort with which you can link your eggs. If nothing else presents itself, sending your news release prior to Easter would make it timely.

The knowledge that you have three news values you can use to make your story newsworthy should give you confidence.

# NATIONAL ASSOCIATION FOR THE HUMOR IMPAIRED

400 South 15th Street
Suite 201
La Crosse, WI 54601

SUBJECT: National Association for
         Humor Impaired Is No Joke

DATE: July 17, 1990

FOR RELEASE: At Will

MEDIA CONTACT:
Stuart Robertshaw
Professor of Psychology
University of Wisconsin-La Crosse
La Crosse, WI 54601
(608) 785-8442 or 784-1821
Photo Available Upon Request

"Thirty percent of the people in America today are humor impaired, and that's no
laughing matter," says Dr. Stuart Robertshaw, Professor of Psychology at the University of Wisconsin-La Crosse.

Robertshaw, who has a doctorate in emotional disturbance, notes that humor impaired
people are "seriously limited in their abilities to live a rich and rewarding life."
He says the humor impaired are passed over for job promotions and lack the social
skills of people who exhibit a healthy sense of humor.

"All of us are born with the natural capacity for laughter and humor, but many sup-
press it during the developmental years never to regain that sense of fun," he says.

Robertshaw, who is also an attorney and an administrative judge, discovered the impairment when a young attorney asked him, "Your Honor, I request that the witnesses be
secreted" (rather than sequestered), and no one in the courtroom cracked a smile.
"Life is too important to be taken seriously," Robertshaw says.

The professor, who gives lectures on the humor impaired for businesses, schools and
national organizations, has formed the National Association for the Humor Impaired
(NAHI) to help those who suffer from this serious disability. Goals of the association
are to:

• Locate humor impaired persons. They may identify themselves or be referred anony-
  mously by others.

• Diagnose humor impairment using the association's Quick-Score Test of Humor Impairment.

• Provide information to members on the therapeutic management and treatment of humor
  impairment.

• Provide information to the public about prevention of humor impairment.

• Advocate on behalf of the humor impaired at the state and national levels.

Lifetime membership in the association is $6. Members receive: a membership certifi-
cate suitable for framing, a copy fo the Quick-Score Test, a membership card and
periodic mailings regarding humor, humor impairment and activities of the association.
Write: National Association for the Humor Impaired, 400 South 15th St. Suite 201, La
Crosse, WI 54601.

###

Your news release might read something like that on page 83.

Such a news release might capture an editor's interest, for there are several angles on which to hang a story. Editors are always on the lookout for new and different story ideas.

---

## SEEK OPPORTUNITIES TO PUBLICIZE

Whenever an opportunity arises where you can say something of interest about your business or organization, take advantage of it and send out a news release. It need not be earth shattering news; something as simple as announcing a significant sale can be newsworthy.

Self-publisher Marcia Hodson found this out. She sent a review copy of her book, *Word Processing Plus*, to home business expert Jan Dean. Dean was so impressed with the book that she purchased copies to sell at her annual home-business conference in Texas.

Speaking about the sale, Hodson said, "Not having much luck getting my news releases printed in local papers, I took advantage of this fact and composed a short one-paragraph news release stating that my book was being sold at the conference. Lo and behold, every paper I mailed it to printed it in their business pages. (My releases were mailed to the attention of the Business Editor.) One editor called and inquired about my publishing the book and asked to do an interview. From that, a photographer came out to take a picture of my office, and I received a half page (with color picture) in Sunday's business section."*

*Used by permission from the *National Home Business Report* published by Barbara Brabec.

---

But what if your home-based business is not very unusual? What if you offer a typing service, and there are numerous typing services in your area? What could you emphasize in your news release that would be newsworthy?

Well, you know that your services are going to get someone out of a jam if his secretary is overloaded and he needs extra typing done fast. You may have been a secretary for years before you started your home business, so you understand exactly what kind of pressure secretaries sometimes face—especially if a deadline is involved.

And what about all those people you help by composing, or at least editing and rewriting, business letters for them? Does the public know that you offer a letter-writing service?

If you send your news release before National Secretaries Week, it would also add the news value of *timeliness*. Your news release could read like the one on pages 84 and 85.

Home-based businesses are a growing trend. Many people, tired of commuting and fed up with corporate game-playing, dream of chucking the nine-to-five routine for a business of their own which they can operate out of their homes. These people would like to know more about the subject—how to get started, what problems are involved, what are the odds for success, etc.

Capitalizing on this trend toward home-based businesses, Home Business Development Specialist Barbara Brabec, author of *Homemade Money* and editor and publisher of the *National Home Business Report*, "the voice of America's largest home-business network," sent the news release shown on page 86 to freelance writers and periodical editors on her promotional mailing list, generating a new wave of publicity which quoted her as an expert in her field.

Several writers who had been assigned articles on the work-at-home movement promptly called Brabec for "expert quotes" (which were always tied to a mention of one of her books or newsletter),

**EGG**straordinary Cre**EGG**tions
834 Ostrich Farm Road
Bergtown, CA 90001

FOR IMMEDIATE RELEASE                    CONTACT: Henrietta Nestor
                                         TELEPHONE: 555-6671
March 1, 2005

                    THERE IS NO SUCH THING AS A HOLLOW SHELL
                              FOR LOCAL ARTISAN

"Fairyland microcosms" best describe the unique decorated ostrich
eggs created by Henrietta Nestor of EGGstraordinary CreEGGtions, a
home-based business located at 834 Ostrich Farm Road, Bergtown.
What starts as an empty shell turns into a tiny wonderland after
Nestor adds tinsel, glitter, and paint and positions minute figures which she handcrafts.

"I began decorating eggs when I was only ten," Nestor explains.
"We were often snowbound for months on my grandparents' farm in
Northern Minnesota.  I watched my Swedish grandmother decorate
eggs, which she sold at Easter time to buy herself a new outfit.
Her eggs were highly prized by her friends and neighbors, and
every child in the area hoped to get one for Easter.  I began
decorating the larger ostrich eggs after I married an ostrich
farmer and moved to Bergtown 20 years ago."

Prices for the unusual eggs range from $10 to $100, depending on
the intricacy of the design.

For further information, contact Henrietta Nestor at 555-6671.

                                ###

**TYPE RIGHT**
**790 Elm Street**
**Bergtown, CA 90001**


FOR IMMEDIATE RELEASE                    CONTACT:  Jane Brown
                                         TELEPHONE:  555-0072

April 1, 2005


                    DON'T SEND FLOWERS, SEND HELP!


Has your secretary plowed through mountains of work this year and
remained faithful, loyal, cheerful, efficient, dedicated, and
punctual?  If so, National Secretaries Week, April 21-27, is the
time to show a little appreciation.  But don't just send flowers,
send help.


According to a recent national survey, secretaries suffer higher
stress than 90 percent of all workers.  Sometimes eliminating part
of the workload can reduce stress by 50 percent.


Jan Brown, who operates TYPE RIGHT typing service, was a secretary
to corporate executives for 15 years prior to starting her home-
based business.  "I understand just how it feels when you have two
days worth of typing and one day left in which to do it," Brown
says.  "Sometimes bosses keep piling on the work without realizing
how much they are asking or without considering that some of the
work could be sent to an outside service."


                          - MORE -

Page 2     DON'T SEND FLOWERS, SEND HELP!

TYPE RIGHT offers an in-by-nine/out-by-five typing service to handle businesses' overloads.  It also offers a unique letter writing service for those people who need to compose business letters, but feel their writing skills are not adequate for the job.

"I've had people come to me when something was charged to their credit cards erroneously and they wanted to let the companies know, but they couldn't find the right words," Brown says.  "I even had one man ask for my help in composing a love letter to his girlfriend in another state.  She married him, so I count him as a satisfied customer."

For further information, please call Jane Brown, at  555-0072.

###

For More Information,
Contact Barbara Brabec
(708) 717-0488

### Let This HOME-BUSINESS EXPERT Help You
### With Your Next Article on the Growing WORK-AT-HOME INDUSTRY

Homebased businesses are one of today's hottest media topics because 13-15 million people already operate homebased businesses, and their number appears to be growing at the rate of a million a year, according to the latest research by industry specialists.

Few individuals in the country have as deep an involvement and understanding of the home-business industry as Home Business Development Specialist Barbara Brabec. She is always available to the media and will provide useful information on the phone, or by mail, to those who are writing articles or books on the growing home-business industry. She also welcomes contact from radio and TV producers who may be working on a home-business segment.

Barbara has appeared on ABC-TV's "Home" show as guest expert in a week-long "Homemade Money" series (titled after her bestselling book) and given dozens of other TV and radio interviews through the years. She is the author of four small business books and publisher of the acclaimed National Home Business Report. "Because of my high national visibility, I receive thousands of letters each year from people already in business or contemplating new ventures," she says. "Such contact at the grass-roots level has given me unique perspective on what's happening throughout the country."

In both her writing and speaking engagements, Brabec regularly shares with others what she has learned from her own long-time involvement as a self-employed individual, as well as what others have told her about their own experiences. Her viewpoints may be just the information needed to complete a special story or segment on this topic.

Now, as a way of saying thanks to the many freelance writers and authors who have helped her gain national visibility through the years, she offers a unique referral service (FREE), designed to put writers directly in touch with homebased business owners who welcome contact from the media. After interviewing Barbara, writers may request the names and telephone numbers of other homebased business owners who can add additional information and color to the story in progress. NOTE: These individuals have specifically registered with Barbara for this purpose.

Because of Barbara's demanding work schedule, she will need one or two day's notice to do an interview and also peruse her database for other interesting interviewees needed by a writer. NOTE: Writers may request the names of people working in specific types of businesses or living in specific parts of the country. Barbara's database information also includes notes on the sex, age and income level of business owners. . .length of time in business. . . whether family members help. . .whether a computer is used, etc.  In short, tell Barbara who you'd REALLY like to connect with, and she'll "plug you in" accordingly.

Again, there is no charge for such referrals.....except that Barbara would expect to be quoted in the article as author of *Homemade Money* (which is available in bookstores) or publisher of *National Home Business Report.* When a "Resource Box" can be included with such an article, she also wants to be listed as a provider of FREE information to would-be home-business owners.

So remember. . . the next time you want to make connections in the growing work-at-home industry. . . give Barbara a call. It will save you a lot of research time and expense.

as well as for connections with home-business owners in her network who might also like to be interviewed. These articles appeared in such prestigious magazines as *Money, Money Maker, Changing Times*, and *Entrepreneur*.

Realizing that publicity for any business needs to be an ongoing process, Brabec frequently sends out news releases to newspapers, magazines, news syndicates, radio and television in order to publicize her four books and newsletter.

She reports that, as she became better at writing news releases, they were more frequently used just as written. One such news release generated an article in the Spring 1991 special issue of *Income Opportunities* on successful home businesses, printed with only minimal changes. On page 88 is the news release she sent.

The news release was especially *timely* during the winter of 1991 when every news broadcast mentioned a recession. Syndicated columnist Niki Scott also responded to Brabec's "gloom and doom" release. After a telephone interview, she wrote a 3,600 word story.

Coverage in Niki Scott's column, "Working Woman," is very desirable, for it appears twice a week in 120 newspapers.

However, Brabec advises, "Never forget the smaller publications. They can also offer big opportunities for publicity."

For example, the same news release was sent to *Textile Network News* (read by a large segment of the nation's home sewers—potential home-business entrepreneurs), which printed it word for word.

As the trend toward home-based businesses grows, news releases on new products and services will become increasingly important.

A home-based business that has had great success with its news releases is one called Memory Makers. The news release on page 89 generated short articles in several magazines, such as *Country Woman, Family Circle*, and *Parents*, which resulted in hundreds of orders for "foot friends."

This is an excellent example of what can result when you send your news release to publications whose readers are most likely to benefit from your product.

It's important to target your market. All news releases are not appropriate for all publications. A news release on unique apparel for dogs called "Dog Togs," made by Flytes of Fancy, hit the mark with the magazine, *Dog Fancy*, whose readers are often interested in dressing up their beloved canines. An article on "Dog Togs" generated from the news release appeared in *Dog Fancy* and resulted in more than 300 responses.

As you have seen, many of the examples I have cited appeared in magazines and newsletters as well as newspapers. Often a business owner who has never before attempted to get publicity thinks only of getting an article in the local newspaper. But there's a whole big world out there, and if a product or service is something that could be of interest and benefit to potential customers across the nation, explore national magazines, newsletters, and trade publications for additional opportunities.

Learning where to direct your news release is as important as learning how to write one. There are magazines, trade journals, and newsletters for almost every conceivable business.

If you manufacture a new type of scissors that cut easily and smoothly, then the readers of *Textile News* would be interested in learning about it. If you have developed a glass to which lipstick will not adhere, then you might want to send a news release to *Southern Beverage Journal*, which is read by bar and restaurant owners. A unique fishing lure would be of interest to the readers of *Pacific Fishing*. But you would not send a news release on a new toy you designed to a publication such as *Weight Watchers Magazine*. Your news release needs to be in keeping with the general aims of the publication.

## from the NATIONAL HOME BUSINESS NETWORK

For A Complete Media Kit,                            <u>USE AT WILL</u>
Call Barbara Brabec at
(708) 717-0488

### "GLOOM & DOOM" ECONOMY SPURS "HOME-BUSINESS BOOM"

With job security a thing of the past, millions of Americans are wondering what they'd do if they lost their job. "While many of these people are destined to stand in unemployment lines, many others will opt for self-employment," says Home Business Development Specialist Barbara Brabec. "In fact, those who are 50 and over may find self-employment the only option left."

Current statistics indicate that as many as a million new entrepreneurial ventures may be launched in 1991. "A lot of these new ventures will be based at home," says Brabec, who has been researching this field since 1981. Now a leader in the burgeoning home-business industry, she heads up her own National Home Business Network based in Naperville, Illinois. Through her quarterly *National Home Business Report,* she regularly communicates with thousands of homebased business owners, editors, and educators in this field, including SBA and SCORE personnel and directors of small business development centers nationwide. "All my contacts confirm that interest in homebased businesses continues to grow," says Brabec, "and many homebased businesses are showing surprising growth."

Can a homebased business survive a recession? "Of course," says Brabec, herself a homebased business owner since 1971. "Many of the homebased entrepreneurs in my national network are reporting growth," she says, "mostly because overhead and employee costs are low or non-existent. And while a lack of advertising money can stop a major corporation in its tracks, it merely fuels the imagination of homebased entrepreneurs who are used to being without capital for advertising purposes. They learned early on how to generate new business on a nickel-and-dime budget. When things get rough, the homebased entrepreneur simply gets more creative, inventing yet another low-cost marketing strategy to bring in the bucks."

In her quarterly *National Home Business Report,* ($18/year), Brabec regularly reports on the changing home-business movement, sharing her own business expertise along with that of her readers who tell her what works, what doesn't, and why. Always featured are imaginative, low-cost marketing strategies other business owners can use. For example, a recent issue tells how a homebased book publisher bought a new car from the profit on thousands of $2 how-to booklets sold to consumers through free media mentions. And the owner of a homebased typing and typesetting service explains how she attracts business without advertising, and without the bother of having customers come into her home. "Strategies like these are hard to find...unless one is tied into a home-business network like mine," says Brabec. "My quarterly *Report* is a unique networking tool and lifeline to others with home-business problems, concerns and goals."

To sample the issue mentioned above, which also includes industry and marketing trends that may affect the growth of homebased businesses, send $5 to "NHBR Trends Issue," P. O. Box 2137, Naperville, IL 60567.

**MEMORY MAKERS**
3024 Haggin St.
Bellingham, WA 98226
(206) 734-9506

# NEWS RELEASE

Contact Person: Silvana Clark

FOR IMMEDIATE RELEASE

Bellingham, Washington--Children quickly learn to put shoes on the correct feet with the use of FOOT FRIENDS. These self-adhesive labels attach directly inside the shoe. When the child places the bumble bee label facing towards the flower label, shoes are automatically positioned to go on the correct feet. Developed by a former pre-school teacher, FOOT FRIENDS means more independence for children and less work for parents. "I find them indispensable," states Sandra Thoma, a San Diego family therapist and mother of two-year old twins. "FOOT FRIENDS help my children get their shoes on the correct feet, giving me one less item to take care of each morning. Delli knows her shoes should be placed so the bee is flying towards the flower. Matt understands his shoes are ready to go on his feet if the dog label is walking towards the dog house." FOOT FRIENDS assures children success in self-dressing skills. Two different sets of labels are available for $1.00 and a business size self-addressed stamped envelope. Memory Makers, 3024 Haggin St., Bellingham, WA 98226.

END

Good sources for locating names and addresses of magazines and trade publications are *Writer's Market* and *The Standard Periodical Directory*. These books are available at most public libraries.

There are also publications which list names and addresses of newsletters. Two of these are *Oxbridge Directory of Newsletters* and *Newsletters in Print*, also available at most public libraries.

It may take a little digging to ferret out the publications which would most likely be interested in your product or service, but the resulting publicity will more than compensate you for your effort.

In this chapter I have discussed several different types of businesses. However, with so many various types in the world, it would be impossible to give examples of how to write a news release for each one. But if you follow the principles outlined in this and the previous chapters and study the examples shown, you should get a good idea of how to compose a news release that will be tailored specifically for your product or service.

In the following two chapters, I will explore in some detail specific examples of the two general types of businesses—a product oriented business and a service oriented business. The businesses I have chosen to discuss are book publishers (sell a product—books) and entertainers (sell a service—entertainment). Although your particular type of business may not be similar to either of these, the general techniques and ideas that are discussed are applicable to most any type of business. Reading and understanding the information in these chapters will help improve your skill in writing news releases and spark your creativity in finding news angles.

# CHAPTER 7

# NEWS RELEASES FOR ENTERTAINERS

Whether you sell your services as a painter, architect, entertainer, or whatever you can increase your volume of business and your profits by using news releases. It would be impossible for me to discuss all types of service oriented businesses. For this reason I have chosen to focus on one. No matter what business you operate the examples presented here will give you valuable ideas and sharpen your skills at finding newsworthy ideas that will relate to your own business needs.

"The biggest problem with being a clown is that nobody takes you seriously."

That is a complaint I heard over and over while preparing this book. Clowns claim that most newspapers pay little attention to their news releases. While such claims are hard to prove or disprove, I don't understand them because I've read several articles on clowns in our local newspaper.

The article on the following page by Della Elliott of *The Daily Californian*, published in El Cajon, California, is one of them.

Just look at all the news values involved.

1) *Conflict*. The couple had inadvertently scheduled their wedding for the same day they were to take part in a parade. Should they reschedule the wedding or back out on their commitment to take part in the parade?

2) *Progress or Disaster*. The article showed how they had made progress in working out the arrangements to handle the conflict so it would not be a disaster.

3) *Consequence*. Getting married on that particular day meant they would not have any time alone for more than twelve hours.

4) *Timeliness and Proximity*. They lived in the area and were known to many local people (proximity). And since the article appeared a few days before the Mother Goose Parade, one of the largest parades in the country, the subject was timely.

5) *Novelty*. Few clowns marry other clowns and ride down Main Street in a golf cart carrying a sign saying, "Just Married," on their wedding day.

6) *Romance and Human Interest*. Despite all the hoopla surrounding the parade and that night's benefit for the San Francisco area earthquake victims, the bottom line was that these two people were in love and getting married, yet still handling their obligations in a responsible fashion.

# Couple finds that clowning around and marriage fit well on parade day

**By Della Elliott**
*Californian staff writer*

EL CAJON — After Lakeside resident Terry Sharky and his fiancee, Dee Harris, get married Sunday, they plan to celebrate by clowning around.

They mean this in the most literal sense.

Sharky, 32, and Harris, 42, are bonafide clowns who will be part of the Mother Goose Parade ensemble, along with several other members of the San Diego State University Clown Association.

It just so happens that parade day is also wedding day for the Lakeside twosome.

"It was just a coincidence," said Harris, who became a clown after finsihing a six-week course offered by the SDSU Clown Association. "We decided that we wanted to be married Nov. 19, then we found out at an association meeting that that was also the day of the parade."

With wedding plans geared toward that day, the pair found themselves in a quandary. They decided in the end to schedule their wedding to accommodate both their wedding and the big parade.

Their wedding is planned for 10:30 a.m., which the pair say should give them enough time to change into their costumes, slap on make-up and be at the parade site by 12:30 p.m.

Since it takes about 45 minutes to an hour to put on their clown faces, the couple said they plan to bring along their clown outfits and make-up to Midway Baptist Church East in Cl Cajon. There they can make a hurried transformation after the wedding.

Harris confesses that for a fleeting moment she and her fiance considered saving a step by getting married in their clown getups.

"But then, we thought since our friends and family will be there at the wedding, we'd better do it in a civil way," Harris said with a laugh. "There's a place and time for everything. A church isn't really an appropriate place to look like a clown."

The Rev. Tony Foglio, pastor of Midway Baptist, said he's "delighted" about the couple's rather unorthodox wedding day plans.

"I think it's exciting," he said. "It shows they have a positive upbeat view of marriage. It's going to be a good time for them."

Sharky, who'll be transforming into Topper, the hobo clown after his wedding, said he hopes to be able to convince parade officials to allow the pair to ride in the parade in a modified golf cart, so they can hang a "Just Married" sign and drape some crepe paper on it.

The Mother Goose Parade, the pair say, won't be the end of clowning around on their wedding day. Later in the evening, they'll be taking part in a benefit at Sea World for San Francisco area earthquake victims.

Harris, who uses the name, "Starbrite," when she's in character, concedes that some of her friends and acquaintances have looked at her in askance when she told them about her wedding day plans.

"I guess you have to be a clown to understand," she said.

---

What newspaper would turn down a story with that many news values? Okay, sure—if you wrote it in crayon on a brown paper bag, a newspaper might think you were just clowning around. But, short of that, I'd bet money that a story with that many news values would get coverage in newspapers any place in the country.

As it happens, that particular story was not generated by a news release. It came from a telephone tip from the minister who married the couple. Even though both were professional clowns and understood the need to keep their names before the public, neither thought to contact the paper about their unusual marriage circumstances.

Of course, they did have a lot on their minds, and they may not have wanted to "commercialize" their wedding. But it was a perfect opportunity for a news release tied to a local event.

Even when local entertainers do not have something as important as an impending wedding on their minds, they often overlook the possibility of getting publicity tied to events such as parades, carnivals, state and county fairs, street fairs, arts and crafts shows, or local business promotions at which they appear. And it isn't just clowns who miss these opportunities, but all kinds of entertainers, such as actors, musicians, singers, jugglers, dancers, magicians, puppeteers, comedians, mimes, storytellers, fire-eaters, sword-swallowers, hypnotists, acrobats, face painters, and even caricaturists.

One such opportunity came to entertainer, Dr. Michael Dean, who had been mesmerizing audiences in this area for years. When he was scheduled to appear at the Mountain Empire High School, the news release on page 93 was sent to *The Alpine Sun*.

**FOR IMMEDIATE RELEASE**

March 28, 2005                          CONTACT: Chico Payan
                                                 Mtn. Empire A.S.B.

                                        TELEPHONE: 473-8601


### WORLD FAMOUS HYPNOTIST BRINGS HIS SHOW
### TO MTN. EMPIRE HIGH SCHOOL

The Mtn. Empire High School's A.S.B. is very proud to present the
return engagement of Dr. Michael Dean, the world's most famous
hypnotist.  This will be Dr. Dean's third show at Mtn. Empire.
His past audiences have had tears rolling down their cheeks from
laughter caused by the antics of Dr. Dean's "subjects."

Don't miss Dr. Michael Dean's return engagement at the Mtn. Empire
High School's multi-purpose room on Saturday, April 13th at 7:30
p.m.

Tickets are $5.00 pre-sale and $6.00 at the door.  Pre-sale tickets can be purchased at the A.S.B. office at the high school.


                                ###

# Hypnotist to entrance high school

Dr. Michael Dean, billed as the world's most famous hypnotist, will return to Mountain Empire High School Saturday, April 13.

The Associated Student Body is sponsoring his hilarious show, which takes place in the school's multim-purpose room at 7:30 p.m.

This will be Dr. Dean's third show at Mtn. Empire and he is well-known for the humor of his shows.

Tickets are $5 pre-sale and $6 at the door. Pre-sale tickets can be purchased at the ASB office at the high school.

Notice of an upcoming event is especially important in small communities where people depend heavily on their local newspaper to keep them informed on what is happening in their area. Since Dr. Dean's show was on April 13, the article above, which appeared in *The Alpine Sun* on April 10, was perfectly timed for advance publicity in that rural mountain area. The show drew a crowd of 250 people.

You may have noticed that it was the high school A.S.B. office that sent the news release, not Dr. Dean. In this case, it probably did not make a significant difference, for he was already well-known throughout San Diego County.

But entertainers who are not so widely known should not depend on the sponsors to publicize their appearances at events. For one thing, the sponsor is most likely to focus the news release on the event itself, rather than on the entertainer. If the event is a large one, such as a state or county fair, where there are likely to be many entertainers, an individual performer may receive nothing more than a mention.

On the other hand, if you will be performing at the fair, it is a perfect opportunity to send your own news release, not only stating that you will be appearing, but giving some background on yourself and your act so that a reporter can build a feature story.

Even if the event isn't large, but a modest show at a local school, it's a good idea to send a news release about your appearance... especially if the public is invited.

Family entertainers perform at school shows all the time. Some do 400 to 500 shows a year, yet few send news releases to the local newspaper telling of their scheduled appearances.

Perhaps the reason is because they do not think their appearance is newsworthy. But it often is, especially if a show centers around a theme such as drug abuse, bicycle and pedestrian safety, nutrition, or anything else that would be of real benefit to children. A show that is entertaining, but at the same time teaches good and useful principles, is something parents would want to know about.

Officer Gary Strudler, of Portland, Oregon, assigned to the Crime Prevention Unit of the Multnomah County Sheriff's Office, has a bachelor's of science degree in criminal justice and a master's in education. He also has a wife and three young children, which may have given him the inspiration to turn to entertaining as a means of conveying a message to elementary school children.

In addition to his credentials as a law officer, Strudler is a ventriloquist, magician, and puppeteer. Using these talents, he has presented information on topics such as "stranger danger," shop-lifting, and bike safety. He added a program on child abuse to his repertoire in 1980. In 1984, he decided to concentrate full-time on presenting safety education programs and developed his own company called "Uplifting Enterprises."

Strudler has had no problem getting publicity for his business for (1) the programs he presents are timely and newsworthy, and (2) the fact that he is a law officer who has channeled his energy into developing uplifting and helpful entertainment for children is the stuff of which feature articles are made.

Since many family entertainers ply their art on a part-time basis and have full-time jobs as doctors, lawyers, accountants, etc., this divergence in vocation and avocation is often newsworthy.

The news release on page 96 emphasizes the career change of ventriloquist Joe Gandelman, a forty-year-old man who gave up a seventeen-year career as a journalist to work with a bunch of dummies. I can just imagine that city editors around the country, having read that last line, are saying, "What's the difference?" Well, for one thing, when working with dummies in his ventriloquist act, Gandelman can put words in their mouths. As a journalist, that was a "No-No."

The news release brings in the news value of *prominence* (because Gandelman had been well-known as a journalist) and *proximity* (because he worked for a local newspaper). Since he had switched careers only two months before, the release was still *timely*. (If the career change had happened five years ago, this would not have been significant.) And, since being a ventriloquist is so different from being a journalist, it has the added news value of *novelty*.

As a result of his news release, the *San Diego Family Press*, read by thousands of potential customers, published the article below.

When trying to publicize yourself or your act, remember that editors and reporters are looking for a story that will interest their readers. Your act may

be superb, but stories about your act may not be as entertaining or newsworthy. So you need to think of some angle that will be interesting. Often, facts about you as a person or your lifestyle will get an editor's attention.

The news release on pages 97 and 98 is just such an example. It is about another couple of family entertainers who got caught up in the magic of romance...in more ways than one. In this case, she is a clown and he is a magician. As their relationship deepened, they decided to form a new business entity together. Naturally, they wanted to let the public know about it.

They sent the news release to publications around San Diego County.

This release resulted in a calendar listing in the *San Diego Parent*, a publication read by potential customers who might be looking for entertainers for their children's birthday parties, for example.

But *The Daily Californian* did a huge feature article on the couple. The story, by Nancy Weingartner, is shown on page 99.

Once again, lots of news values were involved. Both Eastman and Barton had a degree of *prominence* in their fields, she as instructor of clownology at the local community college and he as current president of the Magic Guild of Southern California. Romance was involved, which brought in the news value of *human interest*. And it is somewhat of a *novelty* to have your "significant other" read your mind while you clown around in the kitchen fixing his dinner.

# Former Reporter Is No Dummy

Longtime journalist Joe Gandelman has given up a 17-year career in newspapers to become a full-time ventriloquist. Gandelman, who most recently covered issues involving the border, immigration and North County education for **The San Diego Union**, will be working with 10 dummies. For the past two years he has been a highly popular part-time entertainer locally, appearing at company picnics, restaurants, adult parties, weddings, bar mitzvahs, school assemblies and children's birthday parties.

# Ghost Communications

## (619) 435-7279          January 6, 1991
CONTACT: John Turner, Owner

JOURNALIST TURNED COMEDIAN TO PERFORM AT LEISURE WORLD

Long-time journalist Joe Gandelman will perform at Leisure
World Jan. 16, 1991, in his new career as a full time professional
comic-ventriloquist.

Gandelman will delight his audience in a 7:30 p.m. performance
in the Leisure World clubhouse as he has other audiences since
giving up a 17-year career last November to pursue his
childhood dream.

Gandelman, 40, left the San Diego Union Nov. 8 and immediatley
began working full time with his cast of eight dummies.

Most recently, Gandelman covered beats such as the
international border, immigration and North County Education.

Gandelman also worked as a free-lance writer, covering
political strife in India and in post-Franco Spain. He
contributed to National Public Radio and worked as a reporter
in Witchita, Kansas, before joining the San Diego Union.

Over the past two years Gandelman has been a highly popular
part-time comic-ventriloquist on the San Diego scene, appearing
at night clubs, adult parties, childrens' parties and various
corporate events. He also donates his time to charitable
causes, as his schedule permits.

"This is the classic case of a boyhood hobby that resurfaced in
an adult and then took an incredible life of its own,"
Gandelman says, without moving his lips.

#

## Correspond! 1112 First St. #151 • Coronado, CA

# MAGICAL HAPPENINGS

P.O. Box 171321, San Diego, California 92197

**FOR IMMEDIATE RELEASE**

DATE: March 4, 1991

CONTACT: JAN EASTMAN

TELEPHONE: (619) 467-9596

New Entertainment Entity

### MERGING TALENTS CREATES MAGICAL HAPPENINGS

Local entertainers Jan Eastman and Paul Barton have merged their considerable talents to form a new entertainment entity called "Magical Happenings."

Magical Happenings is apropos, for the couple experienced a little magic of their own when they met at a Magic Guild of Southern California meeting about a year and a half ago. As their relationship grew, they discussed their ideas on quality and professionalism in family entertainment, subjects about which they both feel strongly.

"It occurred to us," said Barton, "that, until now, customers had to call one place for a clown, another for a magician, and somewhere else if they wanted a theme character, such as a rabbit, princess, witch or Santa. We feel that Magical Happenings will better serve the public by offering a variety of entertainment with just one telephone call 467-9596.

"Magical Happenings will provide more than a few simple card or rope tricks," added Eastman, instructor of clownology courses

- MORE -

page 2   New Entertainment Entity


at Grossmont Community College. "It will deliver thoroughly entertaining shows. We also feel that a wide range of costuming is a great asset in quality entertainment. After all, a show at Easter is more impressive if an Easter bunny magically produces eggs from behind a child's ear."

Although Eastman is widely known as Sandy Jay--the Sailor Clown, she includes a cast of other characters in her repertoire: Janna's Jungle Magic, Princess Janna, and Captain Janna--Space Cadet.  She can just as easily turn into an Easter bunny, a silly Halloween witch, Ms. S. Claus, a Cowgirl or Indian, to name just a few.

Barton, current president of the Magic Guild of Southern California, is an active member of the International Brotherhood of Magicians and the Society of American Magicians.  He has entertained all over the world during his career in the United States Air Force.  For the past 13 years he has been entertaining in San Diego.

Eastman also takes entertaining seriously.  In addition to her duties as a clownology instructor, she is an active member of Clowns of America International, World Clowns of America, the SDSU Clown Club, the East County Clown Alley, the Magic Guild of Southern California, and the International Brotherhood of Magicians, keeping her current on new clowning and magic concepts.


###

*When this couple — a "mentalist" and a real clown — got together, something special was in the air.*

Ron Dipping *The Californian*
**Magician Paul Barton waves his magic wand to turn his partner, Jan Eastman, into Princess Janna. Eastman can actually make the transformation on her own, but as owners of Magical Happenings, the couple is used to doing things with a flair.**

Ron Dipping *The Californian*

# MAKING MAGIC

By Nancy Weingartner
*Californian staff writer*

It contradicts the bumper sticker philosophy, but at the Eastman-Barton household, it's magic that happens.

While the 9-to-5 work world is taking a weekend break, the owners of Magical Happenings are at their busiest, entertaining at children's birthday parties or delving into the mysteries of the mind with older kids-at-heart.

Jan Eastman, the clown, and Paul Barton, the magician, have been a duo since meeting at a Magic Guild of Southern California meeting. It was a match made in, well maybe not heaven, closer to Caesar's Palace.

"Before I met Paul it was difficult to date," Eastman said.

Not only was she usually working during the prime dating hours, very few men were comfortable going out with a clown, even if the only makeup she showed up in was a little blush and lipstick.

At the ripe age of 53, Barton has been practicing magic since he was 8 years old. There is no mandatory retiring age for a magician, he adds. As long as the fingers stay nimble and the mind sharp, the show can go on.

Eastman isn't quite as comfortable giving her age, hedging a bit by saying that Sandy Jay, the Sailor Clown, her best-known character, just turned 6. Sandy Jay — the "Sandy" part of the name is in memory of her daughter who died when she was 4 days old, and the "Jay" stands for Jan — spends each summer teaching clowning at Grossmont College of Extended Studies' College for Kids.

Sharing the couple's house are the various trappings of their profession and Eastman's other personae — hot pink bunny costumes, oversized shoes, things that are found in the jungle and completed costumes and costumes-to-be.

Sometimes the pretty, strawberry blonde can be a regular princess and sometimes Barton can come home to a real witch. It all depends on the bookings.

Eastman has the opposite problem. Barton knows what card she's going to pick from the deck before she does, and then there's that annoying habit magicians have of pulling rabbits out of hats. And who do you suppose cleans up after all those rabbits?

Actually, Barton's magic is more subtle than pulling rabbits out of hats or turning scarves into doves. They own a golden guinea pig, not rabbits. Barton likes the kind of magic that appeals to "the intellectual who would rather watch PBS than wrestling."

He calls it mentalism and it "deals with magic flavored by ESP (extra sensory perception), mind reading and spooky things." He no longer does the large illusions that call for elaborate sets and assistants.

The two decided to form Magical Happenings because they saw a need for a professional company that could refer clowns, magicians and character actors to customers.

Most of those referrals go to the two of them, but when there are more assignments than the two of them can handle, they have pre-screened peers to send.

Professionalism is what they're most concerned about.

While they think amateur performers are fine, the few bad apples that pass themselves off as professionals are what worry them, such as the clown who charges too much and delivers too little.

"This hurts all clowns because the professionalism isn't there," Eastman said.

Their company's goal is not only to provide qualified professionals, but to make it easy for people to book more than one act at a time. Previously people who wanted a clown and a magician or a theme character would have to make several phone calls instead of one.

Birthday parties and clubs aren't the only places needing magical entertainment. Magic can be used as an ice breaker at business meetings and clowns can be part of educating children.

Eastman has a myriad collection of characters. She's Princess Janna, Janna the Space Cadet, Janna the Jungle Hunter, Janna the Witch, to name a few. She's also the Easter Bunny, Mrs. Claus and Sandy J. Claus. When she's playing Mrs. Claus, she even brings her husband and several of his elves.

Barton, in comparison, is usually underdressed. He works in a tuxedo.

Both have impressive credentials to show, including Barton's reign this year as president of the Magic Guild of Southern California. The memberships keep them current in what the world of magic has to offer.

"It's not that we want to be the best," Barton said, grinning. "We just don't want anyone to be better." (nrw)

**Magician Paul Barton takes what seems to be an empty tube and removes a scarf.**

During last year's National Clown Week, a number of articles on clowns and clowning appeared in newspapers around San Diego County because they were *timely*.

Maybe those clowns who complained that newspapers showed no interest in their news releases had not been making their news releases sufficiently newsworthy. Perhaps they had not incorporated enough news values into their news releases.

Loch David Crane, a veteran illusionist, special effects magician, and psychic entertainer, knows the value of good news releases and how to incorporate news values into his releases. He has

## PHYSICAL APPEARANCE

Editors receive so many news releases that yours can easily be lost in the shuffle. Editorial content is without question the most important aspect of your release and is what editors focus in on. However, appearance also plays a role. Just as editors can be turned off by misspellings, grammatical errors, or sloppy typing, they can also be favorably influenced by a clean, eye-catching release.

An editor's interest can be sparked by using creative designs, logos, and colors. A picture (photo or drawing) is eye-catching and makes copy more interesting. It provides a visual image, aiding the reader's appreciation and comprehension. Most editors may deny that they are influenced by such gimmicks and that may be so, but it is an undeniable fact that the release will get more attention and therefore more consideration than if it were simply placed on plain white paper with a ho-hum-looking letterhead.

played to packed houses for years, largely because of his talent, but partly because he understands how to generate publicity.

The example on pages 101 and 102 is a news release he sent on a show he was to perform prior to Halloween.

Although the news release did not prompt *The Ramona Sentinel* to give him advance publicity, the newspaper did give him after-the-fact coverage. (And, if you are an entertainer, you know the value of keeping your name before the public.) The article that appeared is shown on page 103.

He sent a slightly different news release on shows that would be performed on October 30-31 at the Mid-City Theatre in San Diego. The fact that Harry Houdini died on October 31, 1926, makes the news release especially *timely*.

This news release is shown on page 104. The release generated the story in the *San Diego Reader*, (see page 105).

In the preceding example, you can see that many of the facts Crane had outlined in his news release were used; but the reporter also did some research on Houdini's life and added information that beefed up the article and made it even more interesting.

However, sometimes news releases are used word for word as written. To illustrate the point, Crane sent the news release on pages 106 and 107 about the Mid-City Theater's production of "Quasimodo." It was used verbatim for an article in the *Centre City News*.

Crane not only writes his own news releases, he teaches a class on writing news releases at National University, San Diego, California.

"I constantly tell my students they must get news values into their news releases," Crane says. "One of the news values I have found most useful is *timeliness*. Newspapers are always looking for story ideas that tie in with all major holidays."

The news release on page 108 is one Crane sent prior to Christmas.

MAGICIAN
and
Master of Ceremonies
3753-B Udall St.
San Diego, CA 92107
(619) 222-2849

PRESS RELEASE DATE:  September 26, 1989

CALL LOCH DAVID CRANE (619) 222-2849

"Spooky Spirit Seances" surface Saturday
at Olive Pearce JHS to mark
Halloween--the night Houdini Died

SAN DIEGO, CA:  Four of San Diego's scariest Magicians will

recreate and perform Houdini-style "Spooky Spirit Seances" onstage

October 21st.  Shows are held at the Olive Pearce Junior High

School, 1521 Hanson Lane in Ramona.  Saturday's "Spooky Spirit

Seances" ticket sales will benefit the Hanson Lane Parent-Teacher

Organization, Cub Scout Pack #645, and pay the Magicians for their

time in performing.  Tickets are $3 under 12, and $4 for adults; $1

more day of the show.  Reservations--call Bill Lawton, ▬▬▬▬.

The shows are dedicated to the spirit of Harry Houdini, the

greatest Escape Artist and Magician of his days:  the "Roaring

Twenties."  Houdini died October 31, 1926, of a ruptured appendix

received from an accident:  he did not die onstage.  During our

shows we will play an audio portion of the 1936 final seance to

contact Houdini--held in Hollywood by his widow.

Three members of San Diego's Ring 76 of the International

Brotherhood of Magicians (I.B.M.) will perform the family-interest

show, which will include comedy Magic, visual illusions, Psychic

entertainment, and many onstage impossibilities.

Loch David Crane will demonstrate both mind-reading and

telekinesis and perform one of Houdini's most popular effects:  the

SUSPENDED STRAIGHT-JACKET ESCAPE!

- more -

Page 2                    "Spooky Spirit Seances"


    Caligarti will enchant the audience by Sawing a Girl in Half,
and then...Levitation!

    Don Hall will demonstrate Prestidigitation and comedy inter-
action with audience participation, two popular forms of Magic from
the 1920s.

    Billy D. Whitcomb of Ramona will act as Master of Ceremonies.
Educational displays, spiritualist apparatus, slides, and posters
of the era will decorate the hall as well.

                         - 30 -

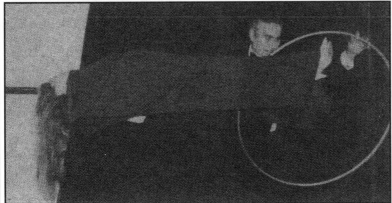

Sentinel photos by Maureen Robertson

MASTER MYSTIFIER—Ramona Scoutmaster Billy Whitcomb assists magician Loch David Crane in his Harry Houdini-like Suspended Strait Jacket Escape during "Spooky Spirit Seances" sponsored by the Hanson Lane PTA and Ramona Cub Scout Troop 645. Charlotte Whitcomb, below, is suspended in midair by magician "Caligarti" during the benefit show, and Robbie Whitcomb, 9, helps his dad, who emceed the event at the Olive Peirce Middle School Performing Arts Center. An estimated 200 people attended the Halloween tribute to Harry Houdini, who has been called "The Master Mystifier." The show, which also featured Comedy Magic by Don Hall, will be an annual event, Whitcomb said.

# LOCH DAVID CRANE

MAGICIAN
and
Master of Ceremonies
3753-B Udall St.
San Diego, CA 92107
(619) 222-2849

PRESS RELEASE DATE: September 11, 1989

INFORMATION?  CALL LOCH DAVID CRANE, 222-2849

Psychic Entertainer demonstrates illusions,
Suspended Straightjacket Escape in series of
Halloween Seances 30, 31 October

(San Diego)  Psychic Entertainer Loch David Crane will perform
unbelievable visual illusions during a series of Halloween Seances,
held 30 and 31 October at the Mid-City Theatre, 548 Fifth Avenue.
Shows will be held at 6, 8, 10, and midnight on each night.  Tickets
are available for $10 per person, and may be purchased through Mid-City
Theatre (▓▓▓▓▓▓) or Magician Loch David Crane (222-2849).

*[handwritten: STUDENT or MILITARY or SENIORS JUST $8⁰⁰]*

The climax of each show of the series will be an escape from a
Straightjacket, performed in the traditional suspended manner.  Hanging
upside-down over the stage, Conjuror Crane will attempt to release
himself in less time than it takes to buckle him into the restraint!

Mr. Crane will demonstrate a wide variety of visual and physical
illusions and provide over an hour's worth of family entertainment.  A
guest lecturer, Dr. Howard Mickel, will also provide a brief lecture on
the life and times of Harry Houdini, escape artist and spiritualist
investigator during the 1920's in America and Europe.  Slides, posters,
and demonstrations of some of Houdini's magical effects will be shared.

Loch David Crane is a member of Ring 76 of the International
Brotherhood of Magicians, and a member of the Hollywood Academy of
Magical Arts (Magic Castle).  He has been a performer for over 25
years.  Last April first he vanished a Harley-Davidson police bike and
then sawed a police officer in half--to benefit the Crime Victims Fund.

-30-30-30-

# HERE'S TO HOUDINI

He started out as a magician and illusionist, achieved his greatest fame as an escape artist, and died a spiritualist debunker. All three stages in the amazing career of Harry Houdini will be recounted in a series of multimedia presentations — four each on Monday, October 30, and Tuesday, October 31 — at the Mid-City Theatre downtown.

Each presentation, billed as "A Halloween Tribute to Harry Houdini," will include nearly an hour's worth of magic tricks perfected by the Great Houdini, who was born in Budapest in 1874. He emigrated to the United States as a child, and by the time he was in his early 20s, he was astounding audiences all over the country by restoring burned currency and cut newspapers, bloodlessly passing needles through his body, performing a bevy of sleight-of-hand card tricks, and more.

San Diego magician Loch David Crane, who will perform the magic in the upcoming shows, says the climax will be a reeactment of Houdini's legendary escape from a straightjacket while suspended, upside down, over the crowd. In the early 1900s, Crane says, Houdini introduced a new finale to his stage show: He would ask a volunteer from the audience to handcuff him and within moments would break free. After a while, "He challenged people to bind him in other types of restraints," Crane says. "He challenged sailors to tie him up in sailor knots, he challenged tire and chain manufacturers to tie him up in snow chains, he challenged envelope manufacturers to seal him in giant manila envelopes. He got out even from locked safes and barrels filled with water that had been nailed shut."

One day, Crane says, Houdini was challenged to break out of a straightjacket. "He took it home, looked at it for a week or so, and then met the challenge in less than half an hour," Crane says. "From that point on, it was one of his most famous stunts. He'd usually do it outdoors in big cities like New York, hanging upside down from a flagpole." Crane mastered the stunt himself by studying Houdini's writings and then practicing for months in the living room of his Point Loma home, dangling from a bar he had previously used with his gravity-inversion boots.

Each presentation will also include a lecture on Houdini's latter years as a spiritualist debunker by Howard Mickel who recently retired to La Jolla after 22 years of teaching classes in psychic phenomena at Wichita State University in Kansas. For more than a decade before his death in 1926, Houdini devoted part of his stage shows to exposing spiritualists and mediums as frauds. He offered $10,000 to anyone who could do some sort of psychic feat — such as materializing spirits, psychokinesis, and predicting the future — that he could not

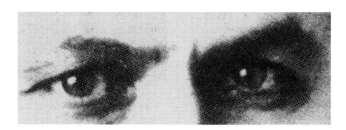

duplicate illusorily. There were never any takers.

Houdini's vendetta against spiritualists and mediums, Mickel says, was triggered by his failed attempts to contact his mother through mediums following her death in 1913. "He visited more than 100 mediums in Great Britain alone," Mickel says, "but he didn't give up until he looked up his old friend, Sir Arthur Conan Doyle, author of the Sherlock Holmes books and one of the greatest spiritualists of his day. Doyle's wife was a medium, and they held a seance in which Lady Doyle did, in fact, purport to make contact with Houdini's mother. She relayed a message to Houdini from his mother, but instead of being placated, he was outraged: His mother had spoken German, yet the message was in English. She had never called him Harry, only Ehrich [Weiss], his real name. That's when he stopped believing in psychic phenomena," Mickel says. Houdini lobbied (unsuccessfully) for a federal law against seances and even wrote a book, *A Magician Among the Spirits* (1924), in which he lambasted Sir Arthur Conan Doyle for his sincere but misplaced belief in spiritualism.

"A Halloween Tribute to Harry Houdini" will be held Monday, October 30, and Tuesday, October 31, at the Mid-City Theatre at 548 Fifth Avenue, downtown. Showtimes are at 6:00 p.m., 8:00 p.m., 10:00 p.m., and midnight each night. For ticket information, call the Mid-City Theatre at 232-9555 or Loch David Crane at 222-2849.

— **Thomas K. Arnold**

# LOCH DAVID CRANE

MAGICIAN
and
Master of Ceremonies

3753-B Udall St.
San Diego, CA 92107
(619) 222-2849

May 23, 1989

PRESS RELEASE                          FOR IMMEDIATE RELEASE

CONTACT: LOCH DAVID CRANE 222-2849


        Midcity Theatre rings in love tragedy "QUASIMODO"


    SAN DIEGO:  The horror of discrimination, the freedoms of

literacy and democracy, and the eternal mystery of love will all be enacted

in a revolutionary premiere of "QUASIMODO."  This innovative and original

play, written and staged by director Charly Fedora, opens Friday, June 2 and

runs on the 3, 8, 9, 10, 15, 16, and 17th of June.  Curtain time is 8pm at

the newly rebuilt Midcity Theatre complex at 548 5th avenue.  Tickets--

priced between $10 and $15--may be obtained by calling ████████

    This exciting live theatre presentation draws familiar dramatic

elements from the traditional film "Hunchback of Notre Dame" with Charles

Laughton.  The bulging-backed bellringer onstage feels the sting of

discrimination as well as the lash of the Evil Executioner during each

night's tense drama.  Deeply in love with the gyrating gypsy girl Esmerelda,

he suffers unrequired love and mournfully groans to a granite gargoyle "Oh,

why was I not made of stone like you?"


                    --more--more--more--

During this important time in history, French Kings were embracing democracy to erode the corrupt power of the church, and Gutenberg was inventing the printing press to spread free thought, free speech, and the hope of literacy to an oppressed world.

Midcity's innovative approach to this familiar story includes an amorous triangle between Esmerelda, Quasimodo, and Phoebus. Quasimodo, played by Shane Pliskin, falls for the enchanting gypsy Linda Castro. Special effects magician Loch David Crane portrays the Evil Executioner. The play also has an anti-drug message when the King explains to the citizens how dangerous it is to get stoned from Quasimodo.

Midcity Theatre is already famous as the only local theatre troupe performing on the site of a former morgue! It has grown from a leased hall to its own theatre building within one year—due to hard work and success. Its director and writer Charly Fedora has a 25 year history of risky theatre and exciting adventures in film and theatre.

Further innovative plays penned and planned for later this year include "An Evening with the Phantom of the Opera," "An Evening with the Music from Cats," "The Rocky Horror Stage Drama," "The Wonder of Santa," and other surprises during the year. For quality entertainment at budget prices, think of the Mid-city Theatre this year. You'll be welcome in the audience—just don't be a "stiff" when it comes to applause!


--30--30--30--

 **MAGICIAN**
and
**Master of Ceremonies**

3753-B Udall St.
San Diego, CA 92107
(619) 222-2849

PRESS RELEASE:  December 12, 1990

CONTACT: LOCH DAVID CRANE (619) 222-2849

"CONJURING CARNIVAL" creates Christmas cheer

(SAN DIEGO)  A whirlwind of entertainment has touched down
in our town dozens of times over the last few months.  Magician Loch David Crane is
"breaking in" new partners for adult shows and children's carnivals in 1991.

1.  Morgen the Musical Clown plays closeup clarinet as he mimes like Charlie
Chaplin, performing anywhere with a spectrum of sound from new to nostalgic.

2.  The Mysterious "Caligarti" performs to haunting classical music with
barehand manipulation of coins, playing cards, and a rainbow of colored scarves.

3.  Balloon Sculptor Don clowns with Closeup Conjuring, and can create incredibly
intricate balloon sculptures such as a motorcycle or Tyrannosaurus Rex!

These partners will participate in DONATING A SERIES OF FREE SHOWS FOR THE
SAN DIEGO COMMUNITY for 2 more weeks.  Here's their terrific Tannenbaum tour:

| | |
|---|---|
| 11-2 | "Magical Mr. Mistoffelees" from Cats for Wesley Palms |
| 11-13 | Ocean Beach Restaurant Walk at "Thee Bungalow" |
| 11-22 | Thanksgiving at the downtown U.S.O. |
| 11-25 | MMA San Diego Toy Run, benefits the Salvation Army |
| 12-1 | On Parade in Old Town; benefit for SD Repertory Theatre |
| 12-2 | On Parade in La Jolla |
| 12-7,8 | Christmas on the Prado at the SD Automotive Museum |
| 12-8 | Victory party for Kobey & Ducheny; Pacific Beach parade |
| 12-9 | Muscular Dystrophy Association Christmas party |
| 12-13 | Cara Kobey AIDS benefit at the Sports Arena |
| 12-15 | On Parade in Ocean Beach +Morgen |
| 12-16 | Community Connection show +Morgen |
| 12-19 | Magic of Christmas at SD Rep; Snow Ball benefits Cancer |
| 12-20 | WELCOME HOME TO USS INDEPENDENCE, NORTH ISLAND +M,C,D |
| 12-21 | American Legion Party; Neighborhood Outreach +M,C,D |
| 12-22 | Hillcrest Receiving Home +Morgen and Caligarti |
| 12-23 | Mayor's Holiday Shelter; St. Vincent de Paul +M,C,D |
| 12-24 | Mayor's Holiday Shelter +Morgen and Don |
| 12-25 | Mayor's Holiday Shelter; Frank's Toy Run, National City |
| 12-27 | "Little Shop of Horrors" Holiday Show |
| 12-29 | On Parade down Broadway for the Holiday Bowl Parade +M |
| 12-31 | New Year's eve at the USO; Whittier Institute  +M,C |

-30-30-30-

NEWS RELEASES FOR ENTERTAINERS

Shortly after newspapers carried the story, he received a telegram from the USO requesting that he provide "professional prestidigitation at pierside program" and emcee a "show for America's finest citizens," welcoming the USS Independence back from Desert Shield.

Crane has found that news releases not only serve to enhance his career as an entertainer but have been useful in other fields as well. When he ran for mayor a few years ago, he came in fifth out of a field of seventeen candidates. He spent less than $3,000 on his campaign. Crane learned that the four candidates who finished ahead of him had spent an aggregate of a million dollars.

What other candidates had done through paid advertising, Crane did through the use of effective news releases. So, even though a magician such as Loch David Crane couldn't pull the rabbit out of the hat in that election, he made a very good showing, considering how comparatively little money he spent.

Entertainers, perhaps above all people, understand the need for publicity. Even the biggest Hollywood stars go to great lengths to generate publicity and pay big bucks to press agents to keep their names before the public. One movie queen caused quite a stir a few years back by taking a stroll down Hollywood Boulevard with a pair of leopards on leashes. That certainly had the news value of *novelty*.

Stars often get publicity when they donate their time for an event which raises money for research on some health problem (news values of *progress* or *disaster* and sometimes *human interest*), or for a political cause of some sort, which could bring in the news values of *eminence and prominence* or possibly *conflict*.

You may not be a famous Hollywood star—yet, but you can use the same methods to generate publicity. Don't bother shopping for a pair of leopards because that one has already been done. But if you are contributing your time, free of charge, for some newsworthy event, send a news release.

Getting publicity as an entertainer is no more difficult than getting publicity for any other business. If no ideas come to you immediately, read the entertainment section of your newspaper and carefully analyze the articles that are written on other entertainers. See if you can figure out which news values are emphasized in the stories. Is there something about your act that involves those same news values?

Are you performing a show that is tied in with a major holiday? Is your act controversial in some way? Have you broken attendance records at some theater or charitable event? Something as simple as donating one afternoon a month to perform at nursing homes around your area can be newsworthy.

If you give as much thought to providing news values in your news releases as you have given to perfecting your act, you are sure to come up with a news release that will generate news coverage.

Remember, editors don't have enough personnel to cover every performer and every event. But the entertainment section of a publication has to be filled somehow. So, if you give the editors what they want—a good story—you'll get publicity. You can make book on it.

And speaking of books, the next chapter explains how to generate publicity for the book you'll be writing when all that publicity turns you into a star.

# CHAPTER 8

# NEWS RELEASES FOR BOOKS AND SMALL PRESSES

In this chapter I will discuss examples for publicizing a product. I have chosen to focus my attention on books because of the wide variety of subjects they cover. After reading this chapter you will have a better understanding of how to get publicity not only for books but for most any product.

Large publishing houses hire top publicists to compose news releases for the books they are promoting. The news releases and press kits these publicists put together are often stunningly attractive and designed to catch an editor's eye. The competition for attention is keen, for book editors' offices receive *thousands* of books each month, all accompanied by news releases or press kits.

According to Maureen Chism, assistant to the book editor of the *San Diego Union*, her office receives eighty to a hundred books *per day*. It is obvious that all of them cannot be read, much less reviewed. The best speed reading course in history wouldn't help with this kind of verbal deluge.

How does one of these 2,000 books a month become one of the 100 books a month to be reviewed?

Chism says, "It's a judgment call... sometimes a very difficult judgment call. We look at a variety of aspects. Mostly we think of our readers. A book on farming might be fine for Kansas, but it wouldn't go over well here. On the other hand, since we're a Navy town, a book on Naval action might be of great interest to our readers, but might bomb in Kansas. We have a lot of marinas, so a book on boating might appeal to the many boating enthusiasts in our area. If the author is local, that might spark our interest. But whatever the book is about, whether it's race cars or romance, the first page has to grab us or we don't send it on to one of our reviewers."

Which gets us back to *news values*. Clearly, *proximity* can play a roll in whether or not a book is reviewed. If a book is about, or written by, a famous person, such as a popular movie queen or an ex-president, it might be reviewed because it has the news values of *eminence* and *prominence*. If the book deals with a controversial subject, you've got *conflict* or *disaster*. Your news release should emphasize the most important news values.

The *Library Journal*, whose reviews prompt libraries all across the country to buy books, receives approximately 600 books per week (2,400 a month). Yet it reviews only 240 to 400 per month.

"Normally," says Eric Bryant, editorial assistant at the *Library Journal*, "only the large presses send news releases in advance of sending the book. About seventy percent of what we receive are galley proofs, most of them accompanied by a news release. Although we certainly don't give a review because of the news release, it does sometimes act as a synopsis of what the book is about and can make us want to read more.

"It also helps to include a background sheet on the author. If this is an author's first novel, we tend to be more lenient in order to encourage new talent. On the other hand, if it is a nonfiction book, it helps to know what expertise the writer brings to the subject and whether or not he or she has had other things published."

Robert R. Harris, assistant to the editor of the *New York Times Book Review*, says his office receives so many books every week that they do not even count them. But only thirty-five are reviewed each week. He claims that many factors other than the accompanying news release influence his office to review a book.

So, while news releases obviously are not the "end all" in getting a review for your book, a good news release can sometimes prompt additional attention.

The following examples are news releases on books that *did* receive reviews. See if you can spot the reason they were picked.

Take a moment right now and look at the release on pages 112 and 113. As soon as you read the headline didn't it make you curious about the book? This book is obviously going to amuse, amaze, and entertain you.

Elaine M. Brooks, publicist for the firm of Lisa Ekus Public Relations Company, wrote, designed, and managed the publicity campaign for the book. She obviously knows how to put news values into her releases.

This release has the news values of *novelty* as well as *human interest*, for the book is certainly different than most, and it deals with things close to our hearts. It has universal appeal for all who have gone bowling, worn a Hawaiian shirt, or eaten Spam. That is a large segment of the population.

When this book and news release arrived at the *Colorado Springs Gazette Telegraph*, there was an immediate response. Reporter Cate Terwilliger says that the book first got her attention because she heard her editors laughing and wandered over to the feature desk to look over their shoulders to see what was so funny.

It may have crossed her mind that this book was "different," but the prime motivation for her review was *reader appeal*. After all, a book on the mating habits of earthworms would be "different," but only a small segment of the population would be interested.

However, "tacky" and "bad taste" are things to which we can all relate. Even if you know your taste is impeccable, you're curious about what "those other people" are doing.

All good writers keep their readers in mind. Terwilliger knew there would be a *large audience* for this book. She says, "Although the press release was excellent, the book itself was so irresistible that it definitely had reader appeal. Plus, the Sterns have high name recognition as authors and syndicated columnists. I knew it was a winner."

Her article is shown on page 114. Considering how many books the average newspaper receives for review each week, this is a considerable amount of space to devote to one book. And this is only one of hundreds of stories that ran in newspapers across the country. The Sterns and their book were also featured in *People Magazine, Time, Harper's Bazaar* and countless other magazines.

Division          New York, New York          Fax 212 207-7901          Director of Publicity
                  10022-5299

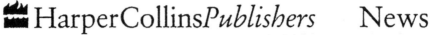 HarperCollins*Publishers*          News

October, 1990

**FOR IMMEDIATE RELEASE**
Contact: Elaine M. Brooks
Lisa Ekus Public Relations Co.
57 North Street
Hatfield, MA 01038
Phone: 413-247-9325
Fax: 413-247-9873

## WHAT IS INSIDE A LAVA LITE?

## WHO INVENTED THE PINK PLASTIC LAWN FLAMINGO?

## WHERE DO YOU PUT A RICKIE TICKIE STICKIE?

## WHAT MAGICAL THING IS SUPPOSED TO HAPPEN IF YOU PUT A TROLL DOLL IN THE FREEZER?

Michael and Jane Stern have the answers — along with hundreds more to questions that may never have dawned on you. **THE ENCYCLOPEDIA OF BAD TASTE** (HarperCollins Publishers; November 21, 1990; $29.95, hardcover) is the consummate catalog of kitsch, an insightful expose including American artifacts of vulgarity, garish personalities and sleazy life-styles. This ingeniously conceived, highly researched reference book gives historical accounts and graphic descriptions of cultural oddities from the margins to the mainstream of American culture. From accordion music to Zoot suits, **THE ENCYCLOPEDIA OF BAD TASTE** "indicates a true commitment to documenting the unique aspects of American pop culture. Jane and Michael Stern are dedicated observers of popular culture in all its forms."—*Publishers Weekly*.

In **THE ENCYCLOPEDIA OF BAD TASTE** you will discover the social impact of artificial grass (Astroturf), Hawaiian shirts and foot-high bouffants. Favorite American pastimes are explored:

**BOWLING**—...the only sport that can be played well while sipping beer from a big wax-paper cup
and eating a bratwurst...

**BATON TWIRLING**—...the stunt of beauty queens in search of a pageant...

**BITE THE WEENIE**—I'll leave that one to your imagination.

If everyone agrees that Elvis paraphernalia, professional wrestling and pet clothing are in terrible taste, then why are so many endlessly fascinated by them? And what about the delicacies of bad taste like Spam, aerosol cheese and Cool Whip — do you know that Americans eat 3.6 cans of spam every second; 6 million pounds of aerosol cheese are sold every year; and one out of three American homemakers buy Cool Whip regularly? In **THE**

***More***

## THE ENCYCLOPEDIA OF BAD TASTE

**ENCYCLOPEDIA OF BAD TASTE** Jane and Michael Stern tell you where Twinkies got their name, why glow-in-the-dark cockroaches and rubber brains are considered "neat stuff"; and the subject of whoopie cushions will keep you on the edge of your seat.

In the introduction to **THE ENCYCLOPEDIA OF BAD TASTE** the Sterns tell us that "Fifty-one years ago art critic Clement Greenberg warned that the spread of bad taste was a 'virulence of kitsch.'" Today, unafraid and unabashed at America's pop culture heritage, the Sterns have put together the ultimate celebration of the subject. **THE ENCYCLOPEDIA OF BAD TASTE** is as erudite as it is exuberant, reflecting the Sterns' unique ability to entertain and educate an audience.

Jane and Michael Stern were feature reporters covering food for "CBS Morning News" and have authored over a dozen books including SIXTIES PEOPLE (serialized in the *Chicago Tribune*); The *New York Times* and *London Times* bestseller, ELVIS WORLD; REAL AMERICAN FOOD (serialized in Redbook); ROADFOOD ( Literary Guild; serialized in *Esquire* and *New York* magazine); GOOD FOOD (Literary Guild) and TRUCKER: A PORTRAIT OF THE LAST AMERICAN COWBOY. They write feature articles and "Talk of the Town" stories for *The New Yorker*, and they contribute articles to *Metropolitan Home*, *Redbook*, *Spy*, *Vogue*, *Ladies Home Journal*, *Glamour*, and *New York Woman* magazines, They also write, "A Taste of America," a weekly column syndicated in over 200 newspapers, and are frequent contributors to numerous radio and TV programs from NPR's "All Things Considered" to MTV and have appeared on "60 Minutes," "Good Morning America," "David Letterman" and "Nightline."

As authors of **THE ENCYCLOPEDIA OF BAD TASTE**, Jane and Michael Stern have been praised by *The Wall Street Journal*, as "a cross between Charles Kuralt and Calvin Trillin." The *New York Times* has remarked that "to cultural anthropologists, the Sterns have no peers," and has said that they have, "distinguished themselves as sort of latter-day de Tocquevilles of American pop culture."

**THE ENCYCLOPEDIA OF BAD TASTE** will charm you, offend you, make you laugh, and enlighten you all at the same time. Thoroughly researched, packed with juicy gossip and startling facts, this "style" guide to our favorite faux pas is sure to become a definitive sourcebook for collectors, scholars of bad taste, and anyone who's ever moaned, "It's so bad it's good." A delightful compilation of the not-so-good, the bad, and the ugly in Americana, it will be published at a time when yesterday's tacky has become today's fashion must.

**THE ENCYCLOPEDIA OF BAD TASTE**
Jane & Michael Stern
HarperCollins Publishers
Publication Date: November 21, 1990
ISBN: 0-06-016515-4
$29.95, hardcover; 384 pages; 8-1/2 x 10"
300 black-and-white and 50 full-color photographs

# LET'S TALK TACKY

By Cate Terwilliger/Gazette Telegraph

Jane and Michael Stern wear their credentials proudly — she an oversized fake leopard-skin beret, he a Lava Lite lapel pin and a leopard-print tie.

Poised over Styrofoam plates at a local Mexican fast-food joint where employees are struggling to bleed the air from a Pepsi hose, the husband-wife writing team looks happily at home. The ambience, the foam and plastic dinnerware, the burrito buried under a huge mound of shredded iceberg lettuce — all are clearly in bad taste.

It's obvious from "The Encyclopedia of Bad Taste" (HarperCollins $29.95) that its authors are connoisseurs of tackiness. From accordions to zoot suits, the hefty, generously illustrated volume includes 136 shining examples of America's underbelly.

"We wanted to include those things that were really like the classics," Michael says. "As we saw it, this book was kind of like a pantheon of bad taste."

Still, some icons failed to make the cut. For instance, Easy Cheese appears in the book, but Velveeta doesn't.

"There was only room for one cheese slot, "Michael says.

"And cheese in a can just tromped cheese in a box," Jane explains.

Such decisions were not lightly made. The Sterns, with the help of three researchers, spent 2 1/2 years compiling their magnum opus.

"We vowed at the beginning that it was not going to be just a collection of goofy pictures of lists of things," Michael says. "We really wanted to research everything. And it's really

hard to research Jell-O wrestling, or Tupperware. Where do you go?"

Occasionally, their efforts fell short: "We really could not get the story on those wall tapestries of dead Kennedys or Martin Luther King or astronauts," Michael explains. "We know that most of them come from Turkey or Morocco, but beyond that, we just couldn't find out."

But their successes far outnumbered their failures. The Sterns learned that Twinkies were named after a shoe, and that Americans eat 3.6 cans of Spam — "the ham that couldn't pass its physical" — every second, Jane says. They discovered that Tammy Faye Bakker's Chihuahua, Chi Chi, ran into the living room and died after eating a plate of lima beans.

"Tammy prayed to God to raise Chi Chi

# Are you wise to the ways of tackiness?
## Test your knowledge of Spam, plasticware and Jell-O wrestling

Cox News Service

What's your tackiness IQ? This test will tell you.

1. How did Twinkies get their name?
2. What piece of Tupperware is designed to combat fingernail odor?
3. If Barbie were life-size, what would her bra size be?
4. A mood ring changes color according to its wearer's karma. What does a blue ring signify? A brown ring? Can you name three other articles of apparel from the 1970s that changed color with their wearers' moods?
5. Can you name three variants of surf 'n' turf? (Hint: beef and reef is one)
6. How much Spam do Americans eat? Which state eats the most?
7. What's inside the Lava Lite?
8. Why does Rickey Stanley, Elvis Presley's stepbrother, blame the King's death on a shag rug?
9. What is a Rickie Tickie Stickie?
10. What flavor Jell-O is used as the medium for novelty wrestling? Can you name three substances other than mud and Jell-O in which novelty wrestling matches are traditionally held?
11. What modern convenience was introduced in Edina, Minn., in 1956 with the slogan, "Every Day Will Be a Perfect Shopping Day"?
12. Name the celebrity who had so many face lifts that he could not close his eyes and had to put drops in them every two hours all night long to keep them from drying as he slept?
13. Who invented the pink plastic flamingo?
14. What does world champion arm wrestler

Bruce "The Animal" Way do to prepare himself for a match?
15. What unnatural behavior did the Rev. Jim Bakker practice when he had his first nervous breakdown in 1966?
16. Name the starlet who successfully petitioned a Las Vegas judge in 1987 to have her age legally lowered by 10 years?
17. In the early 1950s, what added attraction did Las Vegas casinos advertise to attract customers?

## ANSWERS

1. Twinkies' inventor James A. Dewar named them when he saw a billboard for Twinkle-toe shoes, which were brown and oblong, shaped like the snack cake he had just devised (in 1930).
2. The Pic-A-Deli Kosher Pickle Caddy allows the hostess to lift the pickles out of the brine without soiling her fingernails.
3. 39D
4. A blue mood ring signifies "the ultimate mood." Brown signifies a gloomy gus. Black means evil karma. Other 1970s products that signified their wearers' state-of-mind were mood toe tips, mood nail polish and mood panties.
5. Variants of surf 'n' turf include rudder 'n' udder, heifer 'n' hen, pullet 'n' mullet and cow 'n' cooter.
6. Americans eat 3.6 cans of Spam every second. The total consumed since Spam began

in 1937 is enough to circle the earth at least 10 times. Hawaiians eat twice as much Spam as anybody else.
7. The blob inside the Lava Lite is a low-viscosity wax composed of 11 secret chemicals, first compounded in 1964 by English inventor Craven Walker, who named his invention the Astrolite.
8. Rickey Stanley says that Elvis died because he fell off the toilet face-first onto a thick shag carpet in his bathroom and smothered to death.
9. The paste-on vinyl daisy invented by Don Kracke in 1967, that once stuck onto a bathtub or automobile body panel, can never be removed.
10. Lime Jell-O is the preferred medium for Jell-O wrestling (with or without fruit cocktail). Other popular substances include peanut butter (smooth), chocolate pudding, marinara sauce, tepid oatmeal and mashed sweet potatoes.
11. The shopping mall.
12. Liberace.
13. Don Featherstone of Massachusetts in 1957.
14. He drinks motor oil and eats live crickets.
15. The Rev. Jim Bakker took to his bed, where he consumed nothing but a quart of heavy cream every day for a month.
16. Charo. (This retroactively made her 10 years old when she married Xavier Cugat.)
17. Customers were invited to step outside and watch atomic bombs explode in the nearby desert. Many casinos began serving "Atomic Cocktails" (vodka, brandy, champagne and sherry) to honor the blasts.

The news release also helped to generate interest by radio and TV talk shows. The Sterns appeared on 23 TV shows, including the NBC "Today Show" and "Live at Five," ABC's "Prime Time Live," CNN's "Sonya Live," CNBC's "Morton Downey Show," and the "Sally Jesse Raphael Show," to name a few. They also appeared on 128 radio programs.

The producers of these shows recognized that the Sterns and *The Encyclopedia of Bad Taste* would have wide appeal to their viewers and listeners.

Within three months of publication, 50,000 copies of the book had been sold.

That example illustrates what can happen when you start with a good book that subsequently receives lots of publicity.

Of course, HarperCollins is a well-known publishing house and had the resources to hire a top publicist. But what about self-publishers and small publishing companies, who may not have the budget for lavish publicity campaigns?

A success story that comes immediately to mind is that of Vicki Lansky, now a nationally known author and magazine columnist. Her road to success started with a cookbook she had written for a fund-raising project.

She says, "I thought *Feed Me I'm Yours*, which began as a local fund-raising cookbook in 1974 and turned me into an author, was the only book I'd ever write. Each subsequent book I thought was my last. It seems I was wrong."

Lansky has now written and published more than twenty books with aggregate sales of more than four million copies.

Page 116 shows a copy of the news release on one of her latest books, *Another Use For...101 Common Household Items*.

Lansky says, "It's important to have a succinct and professional looking release, but most simply get tossed in the wastebasket if the topic is not of interest to the person who receives it."

She adds, "Most publicity requires follow-up, follow-up, follow-up, though a certain percentage

will just happen if you get it into enough people's hands."

Success such as Lansky's is especially remarkable when you consider the facts about publishing in general. Eighty percent of the new books published each year never make a profit. Only twenty percent are profitable enough to be reprinted.

However, Lansky's books have appeal to a wide audience. On page 117 is a news release sent on her book, *Welcoming Your Second Baby*. The first edition sold more than 100,000 copies and appeared on the B. Dalton best-seller list. Now, several years later, a new generation of parents can benefit by the book's suggestions.

Unfortunately, the majority of books from small presses or self-publishers do not do as well as the above examples. Most have initial print runs of only 1,000 to 5,000 copies and do not sell well enough to warrant a second printing. In fact, eighty percent of all new books published each year never sell more than about 5,000 copies.

Unlike Lansky's books, which appeal to parents—a huge market—often books published by smaller presses have a limited audience and, from the outset, neither the author nor the publisher expect sales to set any national records, regardless of how well written the book may be or how attractively packaged.

The news release on page 118 is a "second stage" release on such a book.

As you can see, the audience for this book would be limited. Even at that, through previous publicity efforts, the book had already been reviewed in two out of the three largest papers in San Diego County, as well as in *In Flight* and *General Aviation News*, magazines whose readers are particularly interested in aviation.

Considering the limited audience and the short time *Green Five* had been on the market when the second stage news release was written, more than $5,000 in sales was quite a respectable figure.

# The Book Peddlers

**For immediate release:**
For more information,
contact: Dorothy Skelly

**18326 Minnetonka Boulevard
Deephaven, Minnesota 55391
612-475-3527**

## ANOTHER USE FOR...101 COMMON HOUSEHOLD ITEMS

### BY VICKI LANSKY

* An A-to-Z guide to multiple uses for everyday items
* Vicki Lansky's popular column in *Family Circle*
  magazine features an "Another Use For..." section

Both trivia buffs and devotees of household hints will have a field day with this handy little book. It brings together a storehouse of practical tips and hints on multiple uses for everything from address stickers (put them on books and tapes you lend out), alcohol, and aluminum foil to wading pools (use to store toys, clothes, etc. under the bed) and wax paper. Under each alphabetically listed common household item are five to ten additional--and in many cases, surprising--uses for that item. For example:

### Another Use For...TOOTHPICKS

* To help keep birthday candles upright, push a toothpick into the bottom of each candle before placing it on a cake.
* Before repainting or wallpapering your walls, insert tooth picks in the holes left by the nails or picture hooks that you've removed.
* Use a toothpick to push lace and other hard to handle materials in place under the pressure foot on your sewing machine.
* When frying sausage links, put toothpicks through two at a time. It will keep them from rolling around and they will need to be turned only once.
* If you lose a screw out of your eyeglass frames, a wooden tooth pick tip will hold your glasses together until you can get them fixed.

trade paperback  ISBN 916773-30-2
15 line drawings,  150 pages, 7" x7"
March 1991 pub date
**$6.95** retail

*Vicki Lansky* has collected and shared her practical hints and tips for years through her numerous parenting books, media appearances and feature columns. Her 20+ parenting titles combined have sold over 4 million copies. Her *HELP* hints column has appeared monthly in *Family Circle* Magazine for over 3 years. She also writes a *Practical Parenting* column for *Sesame Street* Magazine's Parent's Guide Magazine. Vicki lives and offices in Deephaven, MN, a suburb of Minneapolis.

**Another Use For...101 Common Household Items** is available in bookstores or by mail for $6.95 plus $2.25 postage and handling by calling 1-800-255-3379.

# news release
FOR MORE INFORMATION CONTACT: JULIE SURMA

# WELCOMING YOUR SECOND BABY
*by Vicki Lansky*

*For a parent, a second child is a joyous addition to the family, but for a first child it can feel like an all-out invasion!*

## How Can You Prepare Your First Child for the Arrival of a New Baby ?

Vicki Lansky, author of over 20 bestselling books for parents and children, helps new parents with this new edition of **WELCOMING YOUR SECOND BABY** ($5.95). The practical, helpful tips and advice in this book can set the stage for a smooth transition when welcoming a second baby into the family.

The first edition, published in 1984, sold over 100,000 copies and appeared on the B. Dalton bestseller list.  Now there is  a whole new set of parents having second babies who can learn how to reduce sibling rivalry right from the beginning.

Here is information on explaining to your child there's a new baby coming; what reactions to expect from children of different ages; helping a child adjust to mom's hospital stay--and return; good ideas to handle jealousy, rivalry and sagging self-esteem; tips on room sharing for siblings, plus information on how to deal with special circumstances such as having the older child at the baby's birth, adoption, half-siblings, twins and even the case of a miscarriage or a still-born.

Vicki Lansky, whose books have sold over 4 million copies, has been collecting practical parenting ideas ever since her first child was born. She shares parent-tested ideas that _really_ work. Her shared expertise can also be found in *Sesame Street Magazine Parents' Guide* and in the H.E.L.P column that she writes for each issue of *Family Circle Magazine.*

*This September release title can be found in book stores, libraries, or single copies can be ordered from: PRACTICAL PARENTING, Dept W2B, Deephaven, MN 55391 for $5.95 plus $2.25 post/hdlg. To charge an order, call toll-free, 1-800-255-3379.*

**The Book Peddlers 18326 Minnetonka Blvd, Deephaven, MN 55391 (612)475-3527**

## ELDONNA P. LAY & ASSOCIATES

*11377 Fuerte Drive, El Cajon, California 92020 • (619) 442-8782*

9 February 1990

FOR IMMEDIATE RELEASE

CONTACT:   Charles Cordell

Telephone:   579-9072

### ADVENTURES OF A WORLD WAR II MARINE FIGHTER AND FERRY PILOT, GREEN FIVE DESCRIBES EXPLOITS OF LOCAL PILOT/INSURANCEMAN

GREEN FIVE is a collection of escapades experienced by local insuranceman/pilot Charles E. Cordell as a Marine fighter and ferry pilot during the Second World War.

Recently published by Eldonna P. Lay & Associates, the book relives exploits occurring while Marine Lieutenant Cordell was shuttling varied military aircraft throughout the United States. Cordell has long since forsaken his cherished Corsairs. Today, he commutes in his Piper "Commanche" to business and civic activities from his private airstrip on his Cisco 21 Skyranch.

Cordell's book has been reviewed by the magazines, *In Flight*, *General Aviation News*, and in the Neil Morgan column in the *San Diego Evening Tribune* newspaper, and in the *Californian newspaper*. Those reviews, and a military reunion, resulted in 500 book sales to aviation afficianados from all over the nation. The book continues to sell for $10.95 and can be purchased from Cordell by sending a check to P.O. Box A, El Cajon, CA 92022.

Another small press had great success in generating publicity for its book, *Creative Clowning*. Its news release, shown on page 120, was sent prior to National Clown Week.

Though all the world loves a clown, the number of people interested in becoming clowns is limited. Yet, the news release generated articles and stories in many newspapers and magazines, which resulted in increased sales.

The article below by Michele Mohr, published in *The Southtown Economist*, Chicago, Illinois, is one of several that was generated by the news release.

Book publisher, Bruce Fife, gives the following advice on promoting books from small presses.

"Since many small press books are not readily available in local bookstores, it is advisable to include in your news release as much information as possible, such as the publisher's name, address, telephone number, and the price of the book, so that readers may order directly from the publisher. This information may be edited out in the final article, but some editors will keep it in.

"Many publishers summarize important data at the end of the release, such as the book title, author's name, publisher, publication date, ISBN number, and price. A short biography of the author is also included, for it sometimes generates an author interview."

He goes on to say that books are the only product he knows of that are routinely sent with a news release.

"However," Fife adds, "a book will not be sent with every news release, but only to those who are most likely to review it. For news releases not accompanied by a book, a line is added to

# Get a job...clowning around for fun, profit

**By MICHELE MOHR**  Staff Writer

Thinking of a career change?

Then why not be a clown, be a clown, be a clown.

Clowning around for fun and profit is the idea behind a new book, "Creative Clowning" (Piccadilly Books, $23.95), written by eight professional pranksters.

Released in time for National Clown Week, Aug. 1-7, "Creative Clowning" is a fact-filled, how-to book with anecdotes, illustrations, photographs and diagrams that provide oodles of information on everything from juggling and comedy magic to putting on clown makeup.

"This is one of the best books that have come out," says Dorothy "Blab-i-gail" Miller, a teacher in the clown program at Daley College on Chicago's Southwest Side and education coordinator for the World Clown Association.

"I've used the book for my classes, and it has just about everything in it," she says.

And Richard Snowberg, president of the World Clown Association, in his foreword to "Creative Clowning," calls it the first one-volume encyclopedia of clowning ever published.

"Within the pages of this volume you will find an amazing collection of information on nearly every aspect of clowning," Snowberg writes.

The book covers the basics of clowning, including how to develop a clown character and how to apply clown makeup. It covers the history of clowning and gives instruction in mime, physical comedy, working with props, juggling, magic and balloon sculpture. It also provides tips on telling jokes and creating gags and routines. Even stiltwalking and riding a unicycle are included in the compre-hensive, and comic, collection of clowning.

Where "Creative Clowning" differs from other clown books is that it gives good, solid information on how to get a job as a clown. Do you want to work for the circus, a theme park or trade show, or would you rather entertain at birthday parties, schools and charity events? This book tells you how to go about it.

Clowning makes an ideal part-time profession, according to the authors. Clowns can earn anywhere from $40 to $150 an hour performing at fairs, birthday parties, picnics and business promotions. And most of the jobs are on weekends, leaving clowns free to pursue "normal" jobs during the week.

Clowning, say the authors, can be a rewarding, charitable experience or a profitable full- or part-time career.

Hey, what other job will pay you to clown around and have fun?

# NEWS RELEASE

FOR IMMEDIATE RELEASE
CONTACT: Bruce Fife
719/548-1844

### CREATIVE CLOWNING

In recognition of the contributions that professional and amateur clowns make in the spreading of joy and laughter, the first week of August has been designated as National Clown Week.

In conjunction with that, Piccadilly Books is publicizing its new book CREATIVE CLOWNING. Written by eight experts in the field, it is considered the Bible of clowning. The book contains everything from how to tell jokes and put on makeup to performing comedy magic and making balloon animals. It even explains how to set up and operate a profitable home-based clowning business.

Even if you've never had the desire to work as a clown, CREATIVE CLOWNING will make you consider it as an extra career. Clowns can earn anywhere from $40-$150 an hour performing at fairs, birthday parties, picnics, and business promotions. Most of these jobs are on weekends, leaving the clowns free to pursue "normal" jobs during the week.

Men and women both young and old can and do share in the joys of clowning. It's a business that can easily be operated out of the home. Many retired people are finding it to be an ideal way to keep busy and supplement their income. Clowning can be a rewarding charitable experience, or a profitable full or part-time career, but most of all it's fun and exciting. What other job will pay you to clown around and have fun?

CREATIVE CLOWNING can be obtained through bookstores and novelty shops. It can also be ordered directly from the publisher by sending $24.95 (postage paid) to Creative Clowning, Piccadilly Books, P.O. Box 25203, Colorado Springs, CO 80936.

###

the bottom, which says, 'NOTE TO EDITORS: Review copy available on request.' Review copies should be sent to large circulation newspapers, newspapers that have been receptive in the past, magazines and trade journals with an interest in the book's subject."

He advises sending copies of good reviews that a book has already received, along with subsequent news releases.

"Editors, seeing that the book was good enough to receive a review, are more likely to review it themselves," Fife says. "Also, providing a sample review helps an overworked editor do his job. If he agrees with the review, with some minor editing he can use it as a basis for his own review, thus saving him the time of composing an entire review from scratch."

If you are the owner/operator of a small press or a writer who plans to self-publish your work, you will be happy to know that many people in the publishing world feel that small presses and self-publishing constitute the wave of the future.

The news release on pages 122 and 123 from the Marin Small Publishers Association outlines a case for this philosophy very convincingly.

Regardless of the size of the publishing company, the news releases and media kits that will accompany the books on their journeys to newspapers, magazines, and radio and television stations should be as professional looking as you can possibly make them.

For those of you who may have never seen a media kit (also referred to as "press kits"), the article on pages 124-126 by Karen Misuracea of Lagoon Publications describes clearly and concisely just what a media kit contains.

## LOCAL MEDIA

As an author, owner of a small press, or self-publisher, take advantage of local publicity.

Because you are a member of the community the local media will be more willing to give you coverage. You have many friends, relatives, and business associates in the community that would be interested in learning about your accomplishments. Let the media know of anything you do in connection with your book that might be newsworthy.

There are several ways an author or self-publisher can generate local publicity. As soon as you have a book published, let the media know about it with a news release. Make sure you include in the release that you live in the area. You may also send the release to other areas where you have lived.

Continue sending releases to announce such things as significant sales, or to describe how the book's subject ties into local and national news or current trends. If you participate in fund-raisers, speak to businesses or non-profit groups, or help a charitable cause, let the media know. As an author you are in essence a local celebrity, and when you do things in the community it is news and you can get media coverage.

Bookstores are also more receptive to local authors. Whether your book is published by a large New York publisher or is self-published, inform the local stores and offer to have them carry the book. Although most bookstores generally shy away from self-published books, if the book is written by a local author they will consider selling it.

Offer to have autograph sessions at bookstores. The fact that you will be autographing copies of your book is newsworthy and should get attention in at least the book section of the local newspaper. Send a news release like the one shown on page 127 announcing the autograph session.

This type of announcement would most likely be printed in the book section of the newspaper. Most papers print reviews and information on books once a week so send your release to them

APRIL 25, 1989
PLEASE RELEASE IMMEDIATELY
Photo Available
Contact: Karen Misuraca, (415) 381-4601
Marin Small Publishers Association

## SMALLER IS BETTER
### Bay Area Publishing Entrepreneurs
### are Fast On Their Feet

The advent of personal computers and laser printers has created a growing cadre of entrepreneurial book publishers in the Bay Area. As the publishing conglomerates buy-out, take-over and generally eat each other for breakfast, these small presses are responding faster to trends in the market place and enjoying profits as high or higher than the big book houses.

Dan Poynter, keynote speaker at the Marin Small Publishers Association (MSPA) annual seminar in Kentfield on May 13, is the author of *The Self-Publishing Manual*. Poynter said, "We first published this book in 1979 when there were only a handful of small publishers in Northern California. We've sold 45,000 copies of the book since then and our mailing list of Bay Area publishers totals well over 3000."

"Self-publishers and small presses are nimble, they're not bogged down by bureaucracy and they have the advantage of being knowledgeable in the subject matter of the books they produce," said Poynter.

In 1984, recreational biker and mechanical engineer Rob Van Der Plas spotted a niche in the book market when he saw the mountain bike craze start to take off in Marin. He couldn't raise the interest of other publishers, so he and partner Christina Nau started Bicycle Books in Mill Valley with 10,000 copies of *The Mountain Bike Book*. Five printings of the book and ten new titles later, Nau says, "Our distribution is worldwide now and

-More-

Smaller is Better/Page Two

we've just sold movie rights to Whoopie Goldberg on our biography of black bicycle racer, Major Taylor.  We expect our newest book, on bicycle commuting, to catch on well in England, where they've just discovered mountain bikes."

MSPA member Karen Misuraca of Lagoon Publications in Tiburon found a missing link in the book market last Fall and responded in a matter of months with a new directory called *Selling Books in the Bay Area, A Marketing Directory for Small Press and Self-publisher*.  Hot off the presses in March, the directory is already a dogeared resource for Rebecca House Publishing, a year-old company owned by David Waldman, vice-predisent of MSPA and a workshop leader at the seminar.  Rebecca House's first illustrated storybook for school age kids is *Crystal Moonlight*, scheduled for publication in June.

A husband and wife team from Ross, Jayne and Dick Murdock, printed 100 copies of their first book, *Love Lines*, ten years ago, and helped found MSPA.  This last December, May-Murdock Publications produced a fourteenth book, a 164 page paperback with four-color cover and eighty black and white photos.  Almost 2000 copies of their Marin guidebook, *Point Bonita to Point Reyes*, have sold to Bay Area bookstores so far.

"It's the instant turn-around and creative marketing ideas which make small publishers successful," says Poynter, whose Santa Barbara-based Para Publishing company sells books, seminars and mailing lists to entrepreneurial publishers nationwide.

Participants in the May 13 MSPA event at College of Marin in Kentfield will have the opportunity to talk with Poynter and other publishers, in addition to attending workshops on all aspects of book production, business start-up, marketing and subsidiary sales.  It's open to the public and information is available at (415) 454-1771, (415) 381-4601 or MSPA, Box 1346, Ross, CA 94957.

###

# What is a Media Kit?
## Do You Need One?
### by Karen Misuraca

A media kit is a package of materials that introduces and promotes your book or tape. It usually contains some or all of these: a cover letter, a news release, an author's biography, background articles, reviews, a photo of the author and/or the book, a list of questions for interviewers, a current tour schedule, a list of radio/TV stations and programs on which the author has appeared, a sample interview on tape, a reply card and, last but not least, a copy of the book or tape or just the book cover.

You will need a media kit of some kind if you hope to obtain radio or TV interview bookings. It can also be helpful for attracting attention from major print media, in the hopes that you'll get a significant mention or possibly an article.

You may wish to assemble a media kit for the purpose of obtaining sales from book clubs and catalogues, and premium and incentive sales through businesses and associations

*The most important part of the kit is the cover letter or the "pitch letter."* First, be sure it's directed to the person who has the authority to make the booking, conduct the interview, write or assign the article about your book. Just make a call to the station or to the periodical and ask to whom you should direct your package.

*Make a brief, powerful pitch.* Start with a "grabber," an attention-getting statement or an irresistible question. Make your subject newsworthy and timely. Tie your title to current events, social issues, upcoming holidays, new trends and products—anything happening in your field that showcases your book.

The news release(s) should also be concise, not over one and a half pages, preferably less. Use the typical inverted triangle style of newspaper writing, with the absolutely necessary information at the beginning so that the release can be cropped from the bottom up (it probably will be). In the first paragraph, get in the five Ws: what, when, where, why and who.

Remember, the editor or producer who sees your media kit receives dozens, perhaps hundreds, of media kits and releases each week. Get a prompt, positive response by creating an importance and a uniqueness about your product.

Focus on reader or listener benefits and news value, rather than describing the book itself. Editors and producers are not interested in selling your book but in publishing the kind of information and news their readers expect.

continued page 2

*Lagoon* PUBLICATIONS
POB 6322    Incline Village, NV 89450
PH 702 831-7703          FAX 702 831-1337

Page 2

With your trusty computer, tailor-make the news release for each target: newspaper, magazine with a particular type of readership, radio or TV talk show with specific focus, association, etc. The rest of the media kit can be more generic.

If your author's *credentials and bio and the list of media appearances*, is not as extensive or as impressive as you would like them to be, combine them onto one page and even include a photo on that page if there is room.

*A list of questions* is necessary for soliciting radio and TV interviews. It's indicative of your professionalism, gives producers an idea of what to expect, and is of great help to the interviewer who will probably not have the time to read your book and come up with the questions. The list of questions also gives you a chance to engineer the interview to your best advantage.

*Background articles*, by you or by others, may be about your product, about you as the author or about the subject in general, supporting the newsworthiness of your title. Photocopy the articles carefully along with a reduction of the periodicals' names from title pages or magazine covers. Leave the dates off; you may be using these copies for several months or even years.

*Photos* are an important selling tool for TV. And, photos encourage a newspaper editor to use your information because you've made his or her job easier by providing everything necessary. Newspaper editors want 5" X 7" black-and-white glossies. Magazines that use color will want slides. You can get usable black-and-white prints made from color slides if the slides have excellent contrast.

Enclose a *reply card*, a postage paid post-card with a simple form for the editor to indicate if and when the book will be reviewed or featured, if further information, review copies or photos are required, etc. Leave a space for comments, too.

*Follow-up:* Within about 10 days, call the person to whom your media kit was directed, ask if it was received and if it's of interest. Be conversational. Zero in on the most remarkable facet of your product, why it's new, why it's important, why the readers/listeners will want to know about it.

Give him or her a reason to remember you, but be sensitive to time constraints.

If you don't get through to your target after a call or two, leave a *verrrry* interesting message and encourage a collect call back.

Don't give up if the response to your mailing and phone call is disappointing. Regular contact will eventually pay off.

*TV tips:* Find out before you make the follow-up call what time the show goes on the air; avoid calling shortly before air-time.

The sweeps: February, May and November are the "sweeps," when ad rates are determined by Nielsen ratings. It's a pivotal time for stations, and they're often willing to pay expenses to get desirable and very timely guests.

*Radio tips:* "Morning zoo" programs use lots of short phone interviews, and they love faxed-in stuff. Offer to give something free to call or write-in listeners: information kit, map, source list, coupon, etc.

continued page 3

*Lagoon* PUBLICATIONS
POB 6322   Incline Village, NV 89450
PH 702 831-7703          FAX 702 831-1337

Page 3

*Newspaper tip:* Consider directing your media kit to a feature editor rather than the book editor. Your subject may be of lively interest to the sports, travel, family, lifestyle or business editor. The book editor may already be inundated with new titles. Columnists are often good targets, too.

*Magazine tip:* Ask for an editorial calendar. The subject of your title may fit in perfectly with the theme of an upcoming issue. Be sure to submit your material several weeks or even months ahead (ask about their usual lead time) and offer to provide a prewritten article.

The various components of your media kit can be used together or separately over the life of your book or other product. So, it's worth taking the time to prepare each piece carefully, perhaps using the services of an editor and a graphic designer and having it laser printed. If your media kit includes several pieces, place them in a good-looking folder with the pitch letter on the outside.

An attention-getting media kit is one of the cornerstones of your effort to promote and sell your product. And, if you're conscientious about those follow-up phone calls, the free editorial space and media interviews you'll get will generate hundreds and perhaps thousands of dollars in sales.

\#

*Lagoon* PUBLICATIONS
POB 6322    Incline Village, NV 89450
PH 702 831-7703        FAX 702 831-1337

**James A. Morrison**
**678 Cedar Street**
**Bergtown, CA 90001**

FOR IMMEDIATE RELEASE                       CONTACT: James Morrison
                                            Telephone 555-0987
Date May 8, 19--

LOCAL NOVELIST TO AUTOGRAPH BOOK

Bergtown author James A. Morrison will sign copies of his new
novel, "The Baghdad Connection," at 1 p.m. Saturday, May 28 at the
Bergtown Bookshop, 310 Main Street.

The novel, Morrison's second, is a thriller set in Europe and the
Middle East.  A group of hardline communist leaders from Eastern
Europe are exiled to Iraq for political reasons.  There they plot
and direct a plan to recapture political control in Eastern Europe
by joining in an alliance with terrorists throughout Europe and
the Middle East.

Morrison is a retired Marine lieutenant colonel and spent several
years stationed in Europe and the Middle East. He currently
teaches political science at Bergtown Community College.

### 

*Announcement of an autograph session.*

about three week in advance of the autograph sessions.

For an in-depth investigation of book publicity, *The Writer's Guide to Self-Promotion and Publicity* by Elane Feldman and *The Complete Guide to Self-Publishing* by Tom and Marilyn Ross are excellent sources of information and useful tips. *The Writer's Workbook* by Judith Appelbaum and Florence Janovic is a complete guide to boosting book sales.

And if you feel you absolutely must write a book such as *The Mating Habits of Earthworms*, remember to target your small audience by sending your news release to publications whose readers might care. Don't waste your postage by sending it to just everyone.

Markets exist for an amazingly diverse selection of books. The trick is to find the audience for your book, whatever your subject. It often takes hard work to pinpoint the publications whose readers are most likely to be interested in your subject. But writers and publishers are not adverse to hard work...at least, not the ones who succeed.

---

## NEWS RELEASE OUTLINE FOR NON-FICTION BOOK

Dan Poynter, author of *The Self-Publishing Manual* and *News Releases and Book Publicity*, makes these recommendations for writing a news release for a non-fiction book.

**Headline.** Type a descriptive, clever and catchy headline to lure the editor to read more.

**Issue or Problem.** The lead paragraph is designed to invite the largest number of people to read the article. It must have broad appeal; make it interesting. The release should be issue oriented; write about the problem, not the book. The release should begin by stating the problem and telling why this is an important subject. Make it provocative.

**Development.** Spend a second paragraph developing the message. Put the most interesting information first to keep the reader reading. Recite the most important items in descending order so that if some are cut from the end, the most important will remain. Provide interesting facts and statistics.

**How the Book Solves the Problem.** Now move from a "what" orientation to the "how" orientation. It is not necessary to dwell on the book. Anyone who finishes the article will be interested in the book. Describe the contents of the book; mention it as a resource. Continue with some background on the topic and show why your book is unique, useful and timely. Recite benefits to the reader.

**Author.** Spend a paragraph on the author and tell why the author is an expert on the subject.

**Ordering Information.** Give the price and mention that the book is available from the publisher, as well as from stores. List your address so the reader will know where to send the money.

Information extracted with permission from *News Releases and Book Publicity* by Dan Poynter, copyright 1990. For a free information kit, contact Para Publishing (800)PARAPUB.

# CHAPTER 9

# CLUBS, LODGES, THEATERS, CHURCHES, AND OTHER NON-PROFIT ORGANIZATIONS

Getting publicity for a non-profit organization is absolutely essential if the organization is to be successful in its fund-raising efforts and in attracting new members. But many times the volunteers handling the publicity efforts have no training in the field and, consequently, are not able to achieve the desired results.

If you have just been elected or appointed to the post of publicity chairperson (probably at that one meeting you missed), you may be feeling a bit panicky and a voice inside is screaming: WHAT DO I DO NOW?

Take heart, for this chapter will show you actual news releases that have generated publicity for non-profit organizations, plus tips on how to deal with the press once you get their attention.

Of course, you could call up the club's president and say you've just contracted a rare disease for which you will be quarantined for the next year, or that your application to the Peace Corps has been approved and you'll be off to Borneo in two weeks.

But before you take either drastic step (and have to hide in your house for the next twelve months), read on.

For starters, you can accept your new job of publicity chairperson as a wonderful means of getting to know some interesting people in the news media and a means by which you, personally, can be of great benefit to your community. Just because you have not done this job before does not mean you can't do it and do it well. Every single thing anyone has ever done, has ever achieved, has been accomplished by a person who started out with no experience.

By the end of your term as publicity chairperson, your biggest problem may be that you did such a good job that your organization (as well as several others) will want you to handle their publicity next year.

However, at the beginning of your term as publicity chairperson, your biggest problem may be in deciding where to start. Many untrained volunteers think the most direct route to getting newspaper coverage is to call up the editor and tell him or her all about an upcoming event. This can be a pain in the neck to the editor...literally! Think of what your neck would feel like if you held a telephone between your head and your shoulder all day long while you tried to take notes.

So rule number one for getting and keeping a newspaper editor's good will is: DON'T CALL—WRITE!

Sure, it's a lot easier for you to give information over the telephone. But it's not fair.

It's not fair to your organization, because you are much more likely to get the publicity you seek by writing a good news release that contains clear, concise information than by a rambling telephone conversation with an editor.

And it's not fair to the editors, because not only is it extremely time consuming to take down all the information, but it interrupts what they are working on...and editors *must* meet deadlines. Besides, if editors did it for one organization, all organizations would expect it and that would consume all their time.

Another reason editors prefer news releases to calls is because releases eliminate the possibility of errors on names, places, and dates. If there is a mistake, it would be in your copy and not due to a misunderstanding because of a bad connection.

"But what if I don't have time to write it?" you ask.

The answer to that is: PLAN AHEAD!

If you are to be an effective publicity chairperson, you need to keep in mind that you must provide information to a newspaper in a timely fashion. For example, if you want a notice published in the upcoming events section, send your news release approximately three weeks prior to the date of the event. And, rather than putting "FOR IMMEDIATE RELEASE" at the top, substitute the words, "COMMUNITY CALENDAR LISTING."

It's hard to believe, but a club president once called my newspaper at 10 a.m. to tell us about an "appreciation luncheon" scheduled for noon and asked if we could send a reporter. Or take the bride-to-be who called on Friday and said, "I'm getting married tomorrow. Can you send someone out?" Did she expect the editor to shout, "HOLD THE PRESSES!"? Two to one, unless the rabbit just

died, she knew several weeks before that she was going to be married that Saturday. You don't throw a formal wedding together in twenty-four hours.

It's a mystery why so many people wait until the last minute to seek newspaper coverage and are then disappointed or angry when the newspaper cannot comply.

Of course, it's probably that most people do not understand how a newspaper works or the need for advance scheduling.

So, rule number two for getting and keeping an editor's good will is: SUBMIT YOUR NEWS RELEASE EARLY.

The lead time required differs from newspaper to newspaper, so make a point of finding out how many days or weeks in advance of publication your newspaper likes to receive material.

If you have written a good news release and sent it to the newspaper in plenty of time for proper scheduling, an editor may assign a reporter and/or a photographer to cover your event. In that case, you can make extra points by providing the reporter with a written list of names and titles of people who are being installed, honored, or significantly mentioned in some way. Such a list showing the correct spelling of each name saves the reporter a great deal of time.

It also helps the "flow" of the event if the reporter does not have to intrude on anyone's conversation to ask basic questions such as, "How long has your group been established?" or "How many members do you have?" or "To what will the money raised be donated?"

Providing such information in writing is not mandatory, of course. And no one is suggesting you do the reporter's job. But, believe me, this courtesy is really appreciated.

And speaking of courtesy, if a reporter and/or photographer are assigned to cover your event, provide them with seats from which they can best see and hear what is happening. The best place is a front row (or front table) seat, facing the podium or head table. The worst place is so far back that a tape recorder can't pick up what is being said and a zoom lens would be needed for pictures.

Showing thoughtfulness puts your group among those most likely to have events covered. Editors and reporters do try to be objective and unbiased, but they are human. Naturally, they are going to be more eager to cover groups which treat them best.

Of course, some groups insist that they *never* get newspaper coverage no matter how often they send information or how hard they try. If you feel your club, lodge or church group has been ignored by the press, it would be a good idea for you to review the kind of information you (or others) have been submitting. You will probably find that (1) essential facts have been omitted, (2) the information was not sent early enough, or (3) the news release did not contain enough news values to make the event or project newsworthy.

Understanding what is newsworthy will definitely give you an edge when it comes to receiving press coverage. For example, if you are having another monthly meeting, that has no news value. On the other hand, if a prominent figure will be speaking at the monthly meeting, that's news.

If the president of your organization launches a membership drive, that has no news value. All clubs do that frequently. But if the president says that she will strip in the town square at high noon a month from now if the membership drive is successful, that's news!

If yours is an organization which encourages friendly competition for awards presented at your yearly convention, publicity is extremely important to your club. You may want to prompt your organization to hold functions from time to time, specifically designed to get publicity.

For instance, if the president did threaten to strip in the town square after a successful membership drive, she could show up at the appointed time carrying an old table and some wood stripper and proceed to strip it. After all, she hadn't said what she was going to strip, so it wouldn't have been a lie. It would get some chuckles, and it would definitely get publicity.

One concern which is often the cause of misunderstanding between non-profit organizations and the press is the question of complimentary tickets to events. For example, one of the things organizations do most is eat. Show me an event and I'll show you a meal...at least ninety percent of the time.

When the local Elks Lodge gives out scholarship awards, it has an "Awards Dinner." When the Girls' Club has its annual meeting at which officers are elected, it becomes the "Annual Dinner." Various women's clubs have luncheons and fashion shows, church groups have suppers, and the Rotary Club has breakfast meetings. It seems there is a breakfast, brunch, lunch, tea, supper or dinner for every important occasion an organization celebrates.

It is these celebrations that an organization often wants covered by a reporter and/or a photographer, even if the event already has had advance publicity. Its members want that nice write-up they can paste in the organization's scrapbook, or perhaps they feel the publicity might entice new members.

Reporters who cover these events do not, as a rule, have expense accounts to cover the cost of the tickets. Since the price of admission to many events is $25 to $50 (sometimes $100 or more), and a reporter often covers four or five events a week, the expense would be prohibitive if the reporter had to pay the money from his/her own pocket. This sometimes turns into a very touchy proposition, depending on the policy of the individual newspaper with which you are dealing.

Editors on some newspapers hesitate to assign someone to cover an event unless complimentary tickets are provided. Yet, editors on other newspapers will not allow any of their reporters to accept complimentary tickets to an event for fear of being accused of preferential treatment.

Therefore, if you want after-the-fact coverage for an event involving a meal, the best approach is to simply ask the editor about the newspaper's policy on complimentary tickets. If the newspaper in your area does allow it, you may wish to invite the reporter and/or photographer to be your guest(s). Yes, it does take a little out of your organization's profits, but the alternative is to have them standing around with notebook and camera, watching the rest of you eat.

Some reporters and most photographers prefer *not* to join a group for a meal. They do not care to get that involved in what you are doing or take that much time from their schedules. Personally, I've always enjoyed breaking bread with the people I cover. It helps me get to know them better. Often it is the odd bit of information that comes out in casual dinner conversation that adds that certain spark which makes the event more interesting.

If the event is to be held at night or on the weekend, some organizations offer a second free ticket to the reporter's spouse. Believe me, this courtesy is very much appreciated, for it saves the reporter the hassle of having to explain why he or she is always off working at the only times the spouse is home.

But regardless of your local newspaper's policy on whether or not free tickets can be accepted, what can be accepted (and is appreciated just as much) is a simple, old-fashioned *thank you note* when you feel a reporter has done an especially good job on a story. One should be sent to the editor as well as to the reporter, for a thank you note is something concrete an editor or reporter can show the boss when it's time to request a raise. It also reflects well on the editor's department and shows that the public is paying attention to what is written in his or her section of the newspaper.

From your standpoint, a thank you note is worthwhile because it keeps your name fresh in the editor's memory.

It's good to keep in mind that coverage of only one event does not accomplish your aims. You want to keep your organization's name before the public as much as possible. So, if you can get an editor or reporter in your corner, you are much more likely to get more frequent coverage.

But what happens if you want after-the-fact publicity on an event, yet your treasury is at such a low ebb you feel you can't possibly afford to give away free tickets? At the same time, you feel uncomfortable about reporters and photographers standing around watching the rest of you eat.

If you are a good enough writer, you can write up the piece yourself and send it to the editor. If you make it sufficiently interesting, and if it is important to your community, it may be used. If you decide to do this, make sure you get your copy in *immediately* following the event. This is where most people drop the ball. For example, information on a Valentine's Ball that arrives at the newspaper after the first of March is no longer news. It's history. People don't want to read about a Valentine's Ball just before St. Patrick's Day.

So if you decide to provide a write-up for an event yourself, check with the editor and find out (1) if the editor will accept outside material, and (2) when the deadline is for submitting your copy. If the editor agrees to consider using your copy, make sure you have it in the editor's hands by that deadline. And I don't mean "in the mail" by the deadline. I mean *in the editor's hands*, which means you may have to deliver it in person or send it by special messenger, if it is needed the day after the event is held.

Sometimes a publicity chairperson doesn't want to send a full write-up on an event that the press has been unable to cover, but *does* want a picture published...one taken by one of the members. That can be a problem, for amateur photographers often do not take pictures that are printable.

For one thing, most people use color film in their cameras today. Most newspapers print black and white pictures—even the larger newspapers with color capability. To get a printable black and white picture from a colored snapshot takes a lot of extra work, and many times a newspaper does not feel it is worth the extra time. Time is money in the newspaper business, just as in other businesses.

But if you have a really good 8 x 10 black and white glossy, the newspaper may be able to use it, *providing the persons in the photograph are clearly identified.* To do this, you type the information on a self-adhesive label and stick it to the back of the photograph. The typed information should look something like this:

This picture was taken at the installation luncheon of the Bergtown Gardening Club, held Friday, May 15, at the Midtown Restaurant. Shown from left to right are: Mary Gold, president; Holly Green, vice-president; Mayor Thornton Rosenbloom (guest speaker); Rose Bush, secretary; and Susan I. Black, treasurer.

Always identify the subjects starting from the left. Even if there are only two people in the picture, state who is shown in what position.

Your information could be written as follows:

Mayor Thornton Rosenbloom (left) is shown presenting an award to Mary Gold, president of the Bergtown Gardening Club, on Friday, May 15, at the installation luncheon, held at the Midtown Restaurant.

Sometimes, publicity chairpersons paperclip an information sheet listing the pertinent information to the photograph. This is fine, unless the sheet gets separated from the picture, which it often does. Then your picture floats around the newspaper office with editors asking everyone who comes within earshot, "Do you recognize any of these people?"

If you do not have a supply of adhesive labels on hand, rather than listing the information on a separate sheet, it is better to write it on the back of the picture using a soft felt-tip pen. *Never use a ballpoint* on the back of a picture.

Be sure you also show the name and address of the organization sending the picture and *the name and telephone number of the contact person* in case the editor has any questions.

If you do send a picture to the newspaper, do not send your only copy for you cannot expect to get it back. You may get lucky, of course, which is why you list the name and address of the organization on the back of the picture.

The volume of photographs with which a newspaper deals each week is staggering. So a picture sent in by an outsider, even if it is published in the newspaper, seldom finds its way back to the contributor. As a general rule, newspapers keep copies on file of only those pictures they have published or believe they may publish in the future, such as photographs of very prominent people who are frequently in the news. Even with this kind of restriction on the number of photographs kept on file, the amount of storage space required boggles the mind.

Now that we have covered some of the "do's and don'ts," let's take a look at a couple of news releases that have generated articles in newspapers.

Attractive media kits containing the news release on pages 134 and 135 and complete backup material were sent to local newspapers

**UNITED SERVICE ORGANIZATIONS, INC.**

433 E. HARBOR DRIVE • SAN DIEGO, CALIFORNIA 92101-7825 • 619/235-6503

PRESS RELEASE FOR USO GALA

Date:     February 23, 1991

Time:     6:30 P.M. Cocktails
            8:00 P.M. Dinner

Place:     San Diego Hilton Beach & Tennis Resort
            Valet parking is provided.

Honorary Chairman is Governor and Mrs. Pete Wilson.

Honoree:   Mr. Morris Wax - San Diego's "Mr. USO"

Expected Guests:     Bob Hope and Delores Hope
                          Cathy Lee Crosby
                          Alex Trebek
                          Dick Van Patten and Pat Van Patten
                          Lyle Waggoner and Sharon Waggoner

Live Auction following dinner. Sample auction items include: Princess Cruise for two to the Mexican Riviera, and round trip airfare aboard American Airlines to Switzerland or London for two.

Silent auction will be held during cocktail hour.

Dance music will be provided by Dick Braun.

Invitations will be mailed on January 18, 1991.

Colors for the Gala will be gold and white which will be carried throughout the dining room and with the floral arrangements.

For further information, please call Barbara Brown (222-3995) or Carolyn Waggoner (462-6617).

Press packets will be available to those attending the Gala. Please RSVP to Carolyn Waggoner if planning to attend.

Public Service Announcements will be mailed to you on February 8th, 1991 for radio and television.

# UNITED SERVICE ORGANIZATIONS, INC.

433 E. HARBOR DRIVE • SAN DIEGO, CALIFORNIA 92101-7825 • 619/235-6503

## CELEBRITY GUESTS

### Dick Van Patten

Dick Van Patten is one of Hollywood's busiest and most versatile actors, with experiences across the spectrum of stage, screen and television. His career includes over 600 radio shows, 27 Broadway plays, 16 feature films and 6 television series. Eight is Enough is the most recent. He just celebrated his 50th Anniversary in show business and recently received his own star on the Hollywood Walk of Fame. Tennis is his game, along with his enthusiasm of horse racing. He and his wife Pat, a former June Taylor Dancer, have three sons.

### Connie Stevens

A star of television, films and night clubs, and Bob Hope USO Shows, we are all familiar with the talents of Connie Stevens. Extremely interested in the plight of the American Indians, she established "Project Windfeather" which raises the human dignity and helps provide for the basic needs of the native American Indian. One result of this interest is scholarships she founded for Indian children. Miss Stevens' two daughters, Joely Fisher and Tricia Fisher, have gone with her on USO Tours in the past.

### Lyle Waggoner

Mr. Waggoner starred on the Carol Burnett Show for seven years and starred with Lynda Carter on Wonder Woman in addition to legitimate stage experience, motion pictures, his own TV show and guest appearances on other TV shows. Lyle's leisure interests include tennis, motorcycling, classical guitar and furniture and cabinet making. He and his wife Sharon, a beauty contestant winner, have two sons.

### Maria Lee Ostapiej

Miss Ostapiej grew up in San Diego and graduated from Marion High School. She has travelled throughout Japan and has tutored in both English and Japanese. Having studied at San Diego State University, Maria plans to resume her studies with emphasis in law after her reign as Miss California, 1990-91. She has had extensive training in drama and voice and was a featured soloist with the L.A. Symphony. Along with her interest in USO, Maria hopes to continue the tradition of entertaining the troops. She is seeking opportunity to entertain the troops in the Gulf but her greatest joy would be to entertain our Armed Forces personnel after they all return home.

### Cast of Eight is Enough

by the San Diego, California, branch of the United Service Organizations (USO) on its golden anniversary celebration.

Since San Diego County has so many service personnel, both active and retired, who have enjoyed the hospitality and friendly atmosphere of the local USO (one of the largest in the nation), *proximity* is definitely one of the news values in the above example. However, the news values of *eminence* and *prominence* are also present. In fact, the number of celebrities attending the golden anniversary celebration prompted the headline "Celebrities Help Mark USO's Golden Anniversary" for an article published in *The Daily Californian.*

In addition to the article, the newspaper devoted an entire "picture page" to the event in which various celebrities and their spouses were shown mingling with noted guests.

When people read about such a lavish affair, they sometimes wish they were part of the group so that they might attend and meet the stars. Therefore, this kind of publicity can help boost membership in an organization.

Another successful fund-raiser, The Mercy Centennial Ball, was given by San Diego's Mercy Hospital and Medical Center to benefit the Mercy Clinic. In addition to the news release, the media kit contained a slick 8 1/2 x 11 book-sized brochure, which provided complete information on the hospital and medical center, including its history, information on the clinic and the number of patients it serves each year, the names of the ball committee members, the program, the menu, and much, much, more. Yet, it was set up in such a way that a busy editor did not have to wade through pages of type to find the essential information. The news release is shown on page 137.

Although tickets for this black-tie affair were $500 each (alternate tickets were $175), supporters fought for tickets. The ball raised $150,000 for the Mercy Clinic, which serves more than 30,000 needy patients each year.

While fund-raising is a major goal in getting publicity for many non-profit organizations, there are plenty of other reasons an organization may seek publicity.

For example, when the Fort Smith, Arkansas, public library was looking for a new logo to celebrate its 100th anniversary, it sent a notice to school art instructors in the area, as well as to the *Southwest Times Record.*

The *Southwest Times Record* published an article which focused on the library's history, but also mentioned the logo contest.

The article generated new interest in the library itself, and seventeen artists entered the contest.

After the contest was over a follow-up article was published in the paper showing a picture of the winning logo and the artist who designed it.

You can see that publicity for non-profit organizations has many benefits—everything from raising money to fund a clinic for the needy, to entertaining our servicemen, to finding a new logo for a public library.

What is your organization's need? Do you want to raise money for the sightless? Are you planning to award music scholarships to gifted students? Do you want to promote art appreciation in your area?

Whatever your organization's needs and aims, they can be promoted by sending good news releases to the press and the electronic media.

For the novice publicity chairman or chairwoman, this book may contain more information than you can readily recall the next time you set out to get publicity for your organization. To make it easier, you may want to use the following check list to remind yourself of the major points to cover in your news release.

# Mercy Hospital and Medical Center

FOR IMMEDIATE RELEASE

Contact: Donna Guttman, 265-8053
Laura Avallone
Director of Public Relations
260-7077

MERCY CENTENNIAL BALL AT HOTEL DEL CORONADO

Mercy Hospital and Medical Center will hold its gala Centennial Ball on Saturday, October 27, 1990 at the historic Hotel Del Coronado. The Ball is the culminating event of Mercy Hospital's year-long 100th Anniversary celebration and is the 21st annual Mercy Ball. Proceeds of this year's party will benefit the Mercy Clinic. The Ball will begin at 6:30 p.m. in the Crown Room with cocktails and a silent auction. At 8:00 p.m. the guests will move into the Ballroom for dinner and dancing to the music of Bill Green and his Orchestra and Harvey and the 52nd Street Jive. The color scheme for the party will be white, gold, silver and black with the Victorian hotel itself serving as the chief ornament. In the Crown Room the only added decorations will be two large floral arrangements at the registration desk as the silent auction items will serve as the major focus. In the Ballroom the foyer will be decorated with two arrangements the same as the ones in the Crown Room. The main ballroom will be scattered with lit ficus trees and the stage will be banked with ferns. Both bands will be on stage. The dining tables will be dressed with a black under-skirt, white topper and white napkins. They will be centered with a very tall floral arrangement in a crystal vase which will consist of white flowers, greenery, and gold accents. The vase will be centered on a mirror and surrounded by votives. Ball programs will be placed at every other seat along with favors. The favors for both levels of admission will be the same: puffed crystal heart vases in gold foil boxes tied with silver string. In addition to the vase, those who are patrons will receive a box of gourmet chocolates. All committe lists, the menu, and much other pertinent information will be found in the ball program. A guest list is enclosed for your information. Please do not hesitate to call either Laura Avallone or myself if you have any questions. Thank you for covering our event!

Donna Guttman, Publicity Chairman
265-8053

4077 Fifth Avenue
San Diego, CA 92103-2180
(619) 294-8111

Celebrating a Century of Caring

NEWS RELEASE CHECK LIST

1) Does the news release show the name and address of the organization from whom it was sent?

2) Have I shown "FOR IMMEDIATE RELEASE" or "COMMUNITY CALENDAR LISTING" near the top of the page?

3) Have I listed the date on which I sent the release?

4) Have I included the name and telephone number of the contact person?

5) Do I have a headline that will grab an editor's attention?

6) Have I listed the most important information first?

7) Have I included "The Five W's" (who, what, where, when, and why)?

8) Does the event I am publicizing have any of the following news values?

Conflict
Progress or Disaster
Consequence
Eminence and Prominence
Timeliness and Proximity
Novelty
Human Interest
Sex and Romance

9) Have I emphasized the news value(s) in my news release?

10) Is my news release clear, concise, and easy to read?

11) Am I sending the news release far enough in advance?

12) If I want a reporter to come to the event in order to give after-the-fact coverage, have I included a cover letter which makes that clear?

13) If the reporter asks for background information, do I have all the pertinent facts about my organization?

Should you have questions about any points on the above checklist, you may wish to reread Chapters 2 and 3.

If you have absorbed the main points in this book and follow the above checklist, I'm sure several other organizations will want you to be their publicity chairperson next year.

Of course, if you find that prospect totally overwhelming, it's never too late to claim that rare disease for which you must be quarantined. (Better that than Borneo. Borneo has a very long rainy season, I understand.)

Happy publicizing!

# CHAPTER 10

# DEVELOPING NEWSWORTHY IDEAS

As you have read the previous chapters, it is hoped an avalanche of ideas came tumbling into your mind on how you might compose a newsworthy release for your business, product, service, or organization. However, for some people, getting a good idea is the most difficult aspect of news release writing. Therefore, this entire chapter is devoted to helping you dig out those golden nuggets of inspiration that will fire your imagination and pin down those elusive thoughts that will turn ideas into profits.

Publicity is an ongoing process. If you want to successfully promote a business, product, service, or organization, you should continually be sending out news releases. You will want to emphasize new and different aspects of your business, product, service, or organization in each subsequent release.

Since your aim is to gather a whole list of ideas, why not get a pad and pen and jot down ideas that occur to you as you read this chapter. What you are trying to do is tap your creative side.

## BRAINSTORMING

One of the tried and proven methods of developing new ideas is brainstorming. Large companies periodically bring a number of their top people together and encourage them to toss out ideas for discussion, regardless of how bizarre an idea may first appear to be. Sometimes an off-the-wall idea that is completely unusable in itself will trigger a response in another person that is workable.

If you are a business person with a number of associates or employees (even one or two), set aside some time for such a brainstorming session. Ask everyone present to tell you what they think are the most interesting, unique, and/or beneficial aspects of your product or service. *Write these down.*

Even if you work alone, you can have your own brainstorming session, of sorts. In her book, *Writing On Both Sides of the Brain*, author Henriette Anne Klauser suggests "rapidwriting" as a means of unlocking those creative juices.

In rapidwriting, you merely decide on your subject and write for a prescribed time (say, thirty minutes) giving no thought to whether what you are writing is good or bad, pertinent or sheer nonsense. Subjects you might choose could be one or all of the following:

1) Your background and what prompted you to get into your particular business.

2) Things you have learned about the business that you did not know when you first went into it.

3) What personal advantages you have benefitted from, in addition to the money you have made. (For instance, business trips to distant cities that have broadened your knowledge of the world.)

4) Interesting people (employees, customers, or business associates) you have met because of your business.

5) How your business helps people in some way and the personal satisfaction this gives you.

6) How this field has grown (or shrunk) in the past ten years.

Don't be critical of what you have written during these rapidwriting sessions. The idea is not to turn out finished stories, but to get in touch with what you know about your own business, and to get it on paper where you can then consider the various newsworthy aspects of your business.

## NEWSWORTHINESS IS THE KEY

You know from reading Chapter 3 that *newsworthiness* is the key to getting all publicity. After all, the media is not there to promote your business, product, service, or organization. They are there to inform and/or entertain the readers, viewers, and listeners. So the trick is to give the media a hook on which to hang a story.

Once you have something on paper that outlines the various aspects of your product or service, then you can analyze the news values involved and compose a news release.

Keep in mind that in a news release, you are *not* writing an advertisement. You are writing a mini-story.

## CHECK YOUR NEWS VALUES

Emphasizing one or more news values in your release is essential, for it is news values that make a story interesting to the audience. A reporter must include news values in every story. Without news values, in fact, *there is no story*.

To refresh your memory, the news values are:

Conflict
Progress or Disaster
Consequence
Eminence and Prominence
Timeliness and Proximity
Novelty
Human Interest
Sex and Romance

Study this list. Memorize it. Internalize it until you instinctively correlate what happens in your business with news values. For example, if you own a bar/restaurant which holds a weekly pool tournament, and Big Bad Bill is coming from the north side of town to challenge his old rival, Sharky Smith, in the finals, you should immediately think of *conflict*, and write up a news release about the upcoming battle. If the loser will be required to roll a peanut down the sidewalk with his nose, that adds *consequence* and *novelty*.

Study the list of news values until they spring forth automatically when something new happens in your business.

If you get a new chef for your restaurant who has been trained in a foreign country, that presents good story material. If he is an American or Canadian who went to Europe to be trained, why did he go? What did he get there that he could not have gotten in his own country? On the other hand, if he is from Europe, did he have to leave his family to come here? Was it difficult to raise the money for his trip? How did he get by when he first arrived in this country? There's great *human interest* material in such situations. And, of course, any story about your chef will automatically include the name of your restaurant.

It is easiest to publicize a business, product, service, or organization when it is new, but even then there must be some news value involved. Opening a new plumbing business in a city already full of plumbing establishments is not very newsworthy. But if the plumbers are women who drive pink plumbing trucks with signs on the side that read, OUR PLUMBING WON'T DRAIN YOUR BUDGET, that would be *novel*. There's a story there. Who is the brains behind the outfit? What prompted these women to go into plumbing? (There isn't enough money in the world to make ME crawl under someone's house.)

## TIMELINESS:
## A PUBLICIST'S BEST BET

Businesses, products, services, and organizations are not new for long, but since the need for publicity is ongoing, you must continue to find new twists and new angles that are newsworthy.

When the blush of newness wears off, you do not want the bloom to fade from your business. But if nothing particularly interesting or unusual is happening, how do you find something new and different to write about?

When all else looks drab and mundane, you can always fall back on the news value of *timeliness*. Find something that is happening soon that connects in some way with your business, product, service, or organization.

*Chase's Annual Events*, a reference book carried in public libraries, is an absolute gold mine of information that should prompt ideas in even the least creative critter alive. It lists days, weeks, and months that have been designated as the times to recognize or celebrate various products or activities. Some of these have prompted news releases shown in this book, such as National Secretaries' Week and National Clown Week.

Libraries, authors, and bookstores should be able to get publicity during Reading is Fun Week (mid-April), sponsored by Reading is Fundamental (RIF) and held annually for the 2 million served in some 3,000 RIF programs across the country. RIF programs are organized and operated by more than 86,000 volunteers and can be found in just about any setting where children congregate, such as schools, libraries, and day care centers. During this week, RIF programs are encouraged to conduct reading activities which underscore the fun of reading.

A variety of businesses could get good mileage out of National Anti-Boredom Month (July), National Magic Day (October 31), and National Juggling Day (mid-June).

National Children's Book Week (mid-November) would be a perfect time for the author of children's books to arrange book signing engagements to maximize publicity opportunities.

There is even a National Grouch Day (mid-October), but I doubt if most people would want their products or services tied in with that. But if you have a product that could fit, it might make an interesting *novelty* story.

Every single month of the year presents countless opportunities for publicity connected with one of the *thousands* of specially designated days, weeks, and months.

Pet store owners might want to write a news release in connection with National Adopt A Dog Month (October).

Someone who owns a lingerie shop might write a news release for National Romance Month (February), on how frilly lingerie can add zest to a romantic evening. You do not have to wait until February for such publicity; there is another opportunity for a tie-in with National Romance: Sweetest Day, on October 19.

If you own a beauty salon, take advantage of the fact that January is National Careers in Cosmetology Month. Of course, it is also designated as: National Eye Health Care Month, National Fiber Focus Month (recognizing contributions fiber makes toward maintaining good health), National Hobby Month, National Oatmeal Month: National Prune Breakfast Month, and National Soup Month.

*Chase's Annual Events* also carries listings of famous persons' birthdays, as well as anniversaries of significant events, such as the First Trans-Atlantic Flight.

The possibilities are endless. The news release on the following page illustrates how publicity can be generated for your business by using such a tie-in with an annual event.

Fun Mail Week would seem, at first glance, to have nothing to do with book publishing. But by sending the news release and furnishing a free copy of the *Fun Mail Directory*, Java Publishing Company's name was mentioned in the resulting newspaper stories. In addition, those who sent for a free copy of the directory expanded the list of potential customers for future books. Page 144 shows some of the many articles resulting from this release.

So, if you are stuck for an idea, check out *Chase's Annual Events*. There is an idea in there somewhere for everyone. The directory is updated and a new edition published each year. It is important that you refer to the edition in the same year you plan to publicize your business or product because many of the dates change from year to year. For example, if National Juggling Week was June 13-19 one year, it may be June 14-20 the next. You do not want to send out news releases indicating incorrect dates!

## CURRENT EVENTS

There is another aspect to using the news value of timeliness that is often overlooked. That is the tie-in with whatever is *big news* at the moment.

Often a product or service that is otherwise mundane and uninteresting becomes newsworthy when associated with whatever is making headlines at the time. Stores selling sporting goods would have a tie-in with the Olympics, the World Series, and the Super Bowl. Insurance companies had a chance for a series of news releases in connection with the eruption of Mount St. Helens and the San Francisco earthquake. (Insurance agents could have written news releases for their papers tied in with these same events.)

Banks and other financial institutions might want to capitalize on the changing economic conditions due to the fall of communism in Eastern Europe, pointing out in their news releases how solid our own currency remains.

The large oil companies sent out volumes of news releases during Operation Desert Storm. But how did this event affect the little guy who owns the gas station on the corner? It would have been the perfect time for the station owner to write a news release about his business.

Draw a connection between what is happening currently in the news and your product. Each day something new is happening. If you look carefully and use a little creative thinking, you will find an endless number of tie-ins with your business. In this way, you can have continuing publicity for a business, product, service, or organization that is no longer regarded as being new.

**JAVA PUBLISHING COMPANY**
**P.O. BOX 25203**
**COLORADO SPRINGS, CO 80936**

# NEWS RELEASE

FOR IMMEDIATE RELEASE
CONTACT: SUSAN WALKER
719/549-1844

### FUN MAIL

Have you ever felt the excitement of opening your mailbox and finding an unexpected package or letter? Most everyone enjoys the anticipation and discovery of finding something in their mailbox. To many people, receiving mail is one of the highlights of their day. In a sense, opening these "gifts" is like a miniture Christmas. Receiving mail is fun!

To promote and encourage fun mail, March 13-19 has been designated as Fun Mail Week. In recognition of Fun Mail Week, Java Publishing Company has published a Fun Mail Directory. This directory contains the names and addresses of companies who are offering free or almost free product samples. The wide variety of merchandise available includes: jewelry, stamps and coins, puzzles, candy, shampoo, stationery, games, toys, books, and pamphlets.

Books cover a wide variety of subjects ranging from sports and nature activities to do-it-yourself and how-to projects.

To receive a free copy of the Fun Mail Directory, send a stamped self-addressed envelope to Fun Mail, c/o Java Publishing Company, P.O. Box 25203, Colorado Springs, CO 80936.

###

### In the mailbox

Java Publishing Company has published a Fun Mail Directory, listing companies that offer free or almost-free product samples such as jewelry, candy, stationary, toys and books. As part of the promotion, Java says that March 13 to 19 has been designated as Fun Mail Week. Its directory is available free by sending a stamped, self-addressed envelope to Java Publishing, P.O. Box 25203, Colorado Springs, Colorado 80936.

**Fun mail:** Java Publishing Company is offering a Fun Mail Directory. This directory contains the names and addresses of companies offering free or almost free product samples. A wide variety of merchandise is available. To receive your free copy send a stamped self-addressed envelope to: Fun Mail, c/o Java Publishing Company, P.O. ~~25203, Colorado Springs, Colo. 80936.~~

### Directory of freebies through mail issued

Looking for some freebies?

In honor of "Fun Mail Week" next week (so proclaimed by the Letter Enjoyers Association), a Colorado publisher is offering consumers a free ~~pa~~mphlet that lists companies and agencies that are offering free and ~~a~~lmost-free" products through the mails.

The listings include a rubber Oscar Meyer wiener, a Famous Amos ~~zoo,~~ reproduction Confederate money, a book on boomerangs and a guide ~~on~~ kiting.

Some of the items are being offered by government agencies, while ~~oth~~ers are being offered by companies and ~~asso~~ciations as promotional ~~items.~~

All the ~~items~~ ...

### Fun with junk mail

Now available, a free copy of the Fun Mail Directory, which contains names and addresses of companies offering free or almost free product samples. To get this directory, send a stamped, self-addressed envelope to: Fun Mail, c/o Java Publishing Co. P.O. Box 25203, Colorado Springs, Colo. 80936.

~~...tion of the offer for the ...hlet.~~
~~...btained by sending a ... Fun Mail, c/o Java ...olo. 80936.~~

## BOTTOM LINE: MR. POSTMAN PLEASED

Each of us has known the delight of opening the mailbox and finding an unexpected gift or letter. Only problem is, it doesn't happen often enough.

Enter Fun Mail Week, March 13-19, from the Letter Enjoyers Association, a Brooklyn Center, Minn. group that encourages letter-sending for fun.

"To help promote Fun Mail Week, we are giving away a Fun Mail Directory of things associations and companies across the country are giving away free or almost free," explained Bruce Fife of Java Publishing Company in Colorado Springs, Colo. "Most of the stuff is free. A few things are $2, but that's about as much as anything costs. You can get jewelry, coins, puzzles, candy, shampoo, stationery and books that cover a grange of subjects, from sports to nature activities. You can also get a giant, inflatable hot dog and a treasure map of the East Coast that shows where buried treasures are supposed to be."

To get the Fun Mail Directory, send a Stamped, self-addressed envelope to: Fun Mail, c/o Java Publishing Company, P.O. Box 25203, Colorado Springs, Colo. 80936.

Have fun!

*By Carol Teegardin*

~~...ge or letter.~~ Opening these 'gifts' is like a miniature Christmas. Receiving mail is fun."

Do I sense that we're avoiding the J ~~...rd~~ here?

~~... o~~f Fun Mail Week is to ~~...~~ ~~en~~courage fun mail." And ~~... fr~~ee Fun Mail Directory, ~~... n~~ames and addresses of ~~... who~~ are offering free or al~~most~~ ~~sa~~mples. The wide variety ~~...~~ available includes jewelry, ~~...~~ ~~coins~~, puzzles, candy, shampoo, ~~... g~~ames, toys, books and pam~~phlets.~~

~~... st~~amped, self-addressed envelop~~e to: Fun Mai~~l, c/o Java Publishing, P.O. Box ~~...C~~olorado Springs, Colo. 80936.

~~...W~~eek arrives

~~...~~19 has been designated "Fun ~~Mail Week by~~ the Letter Enjoyers Associa~~tion of Brooklyn~~ Center, Minn.

~~... Publis~~hing Co. of Colorado Springs is offering a free Fun Mail Directory to people who write and include a self-addressed and stamped envelope. The directory contains the names and addresses of companies that offer free or almost free product samples. Write: Fun Mail, Java Publishing Co., P.O. Box 25203, Colorado Springs, Colo. 80936.

### CAN JUNK MAIL BE FUN?

Java Publishing Co. apparently thinks so. Although the whos and whys behind it are unknown, next week has been designated Fun Mail Week. In recogtnition of that, Java is distributing free copies of a "Fun Mail Directory," with the names and addresses of companies offering free or inexpensive samples of jewelry, stamps and coins, candy, toys, books and more. To receive a free copy, send a stamped, self-addressed envelope to Fun Mail, in care of Java Publishing Co., P.O. Box 25203, Colorado Springs, Colo. 80936.

### Fun Mail Directory

The "Fun Mail Directory," a list of names and addresses of companies that offer free or low-priced product samples of jewelry, stamps, coins, puzzles, candy, shampoo, stationery, games, toys, books and literature is available by sending a stamped, self-addressed envelope to Fun Mail, c/o Java Publishing CO., P.O. Box 25203, Colorado Springs, Colo. 80936.

A free copy of t~~he Fun M~~ail Directory can be obtained by sending a stamped, self-addressed, business-sized envelope to: Fun Mail, c/o Java Publishing Co., P.O. Box 25203, Colorado Springs, Colo. 80936.

## TRENDS

Popular trends (another aspect of timeliness) can also add newsworthiness to a subject. For example, ecology, conservation and recycling have been in the spotlight for some time now.

A while back, I was assigned to cover the installation luncheon of the El Cajon Women's Club. The lady who was being installed as president of the club had served in that office twice before. She laughingly said to me, "Well, you know how big our club is on recycling."

The remark gave me the perfect hook on which to hang a story. The following is part of what I wrote:

> This past year, according to President Donna Roll, the El Cajon Women's Club has recycled 21,747 pounds of paper and aluminum cans; 2,870 glass bottles; 2,279 pounds of clothes—and one president.

If yours is a business that does any recycling, it could be a perfect opportunity for a news release. Years ago, before recycling was on everyone's mind, I owned a bar/restaurant. We saved the grease cleaned off the grill from frying hamburgers and sold barrels of it to a firm which manufactured cold cream. (Yes, ladies, it's true. But don't think about that. Just concentrate on the results.) In today's climate, with some additional research to learn how much it saved the cold cream company in processing costs to use recycled grease, that fact could have been used in a news release.

## USE OF CELEBRITY STATUS

Don't overlook associations with famous people, such as actors, singers, athletes, politicians, and even local TV newscasters and disc jockeys.

The news values of *eminence* and *prominence* can be what makes your release newsworthy.

A restaurant/bar in San Diego, called "The Kansas City Barbecue," got lots of publicity after a scene for "Top Gun" was shot on its premises. I have no way of knowing for sure, but I'll bet there was many a young lady who dropped by to sit on the stool Tom Cruise had once sat upon.

Not only did its association with the movie get wide local newspaper coverage for The Kansas City Barbecue, but, lest people forget after a time, the management put a sign in the window, stating: SITE OF THE SLEAZY BAR SCENE IN "TOP GUN."

If you can get a local celebrity to attend a grand opening, charity bazaar, or fund-raiser, you have added something that is newsworthy. Many local politicians, athletes, disc jockeys, and others will gladly donate their time to attend a worthwhile cause for charity. They can be invited to be the guest of honor, to present an award to an outstanding individual, or to receive an award themselves from the organization. Inviting celebrities to participate with you is an excellent way for a non-profit organization to generate publicity.

A business can also entice celebrities to attend an event. They may be sponsoring a worthy cause or charitable fund-raiser. Big businesses know the advantage of using celebrities to endorse their products. If you can get a well-known person tied into your product, business, or event, you have a news hook a reporter can hang a story on.

## EXPERIENCE LEADS TO EXPERTISE

Ideas are where you find them, but you won't find anything without looking. The first place to start looking is in your own mind. If you train your mind to be on the lookout for ideas that can be used to publicize your business, product, service, or organization, you'll be amazed at what will come to you.

Believe it or not, you will get better at recognizing and incorporating news values to publicize yourself, your business, or your organization as you practice, and ideas will start coming more easily as you gain experience.

If you have a chance to be interviewed, take note of the questions the reporter asks you. That will help you zero in on aspects of your business or organization that are newsworthy. Reporters have experience in digging out news values. The reporter's questions will guide you in your future news releases.

When I first became a reporter, my biggest problem was not the writing, but learning how to ask the right questions. On one occasion, I was assigned to cover a wood carvers' exhibit. I knew *nothing* about wood carving and had no idea of what to ask. In a panic, I stopped by my editor's desk before I left for the exhibit and told her that I was drawing a blank.

She rattled off a string of questions I could use, such as: How did you get into wood carving? How many years have you been doing it? Do you have a particular theme in your work? What is your favorite wood? How many hours does the average piece take you to finish? What kind of tools are used to create special effects? How much money does the average piece sell for? Is there a large market for wood carvings? Have you sold any to famous people?

The list went on and on. I looked at her in amazement and said, "How do you do that?"

"Experience, my dear," she replied. "Years and years of experience."

She was right. With experience I got to the point where I, too, could think of a string of questions, regardless of the subject.

With experience, you will learn to ask yourself the right questions that will generate newsworthy ideas. So, keep practicing. The skill will come to you.

The next chapter gives some additional useful tips on how to make the most of the ideas you find.

# CHAPTER 11

# ADDITIONAL USEFUL TIPS

Now that you have your list of good ideas and are ready to compose your news release, here are some additional tips that will help you make it better.

## KEEP THE AUDIENCE IN MIND

I realize that I have said this in previous chapters, but it is of great importance that you keep the reader, viewer, or listener in mind when composing news releases and in directing those releases to the proper media outlets.

As you saw from quotes from various editors throughout the book, a news release must have some relevance to the media's readers or listeners. Some material that would interest an audience in some sections of the country would hold no interest for people in other sections.

New ways to combat the boll weevil would be of great interest to readers in sections of California and across the cotton belt in the South. But farmers in Maine or Washington would not care a whit. A financial report of a privately owned company in New Jersey would hold no interest

for the people of Nebraska. Analyze the type of people you are trying to reach. Are they parents, senior citizens, union members, car enthusiasts, jet-setters, or just ordinary, average people? Then find the publications or electronic media stations your targeted audience is most likely to read, view, or listen to.

Don't waste your postage by sending news releases to inappropriate media sources.

## FACTS AND FIGURES

Since the media's purpose is to inform, educate, and/or entertain its audience, the use of facts, figures, and statistics in your news release can work to your advantage. Providing numbers gives editors hard facts. And big numbers are more impressive and more significant than little numbers.

If the man who owned the corner gas station knew how many gallons of gas he normally pumped and how many more or less he pumped during Operation Desert Storm or some other crisis, that would add interest to a piece about his business.

In the example that I gave in Chapter 10 on the recycled president, you will notice that I didn't just write that the club had recycled paper and aluminum cans, glass bottles, and clothing. That's dull. But when I added the numbers of how many bottles and pounds of clothes, etc., it made the point more relevant.

Adding numbers and or descriptive quantitative comparisons can make your news release more interesting and help an editor or program director understand the importance of the information you are providing.

## ACCURACY

It's not enough just to come up with interesting facts and figures. You must make sure that the facts and figures you include in your news release are accurate.

The media is going to publish what you give them. Editors depend on your providing factual information. If you have been sloppy in your information gathering or have just plain embellished the facts, someone out there is going to know and is going to write a letter to the editor and complain. Your credibility goes right down the drain, and the editor will not be receptive to future news releases you may send.

And while we are on the subject of accuracy, make sure your spelling and punctuation are accurate. Otherwise, you make yourself look amateurish, and your news release receives less attention. (You may be an amateur, but you don't have to write like one.)

## NEWS, NOT A COMMERCIAL

If you are writing a news release about yourself, your business, product, service, or organization, *keep out of it*! Do not use the word "I." Write your news release in the third person, as if you were someone else writing about you.

Remember, your news release is a mini-story, not an advertisement. Therefore, also avoid words like "you" and "your," for these are advertising words. For example, rather than saying "You will look ten years younger by using this product," say, "The manufacturer claims that users can look ten years younger by using this product." Replace the word "you" with "consumers," "parents," "businesspeople," etc.

Also avoid flowery words and phrases used in advertising, such as "fantastic results," "you will be absolutely delighted," "nobody beats our prices," "best product on the market," etc. They tend to turn an editor off.

Editors normally toss out news releases that are blatantly commercial. So, even though publicizing your business may be your aim, focus on an idea that will interest and benefit the audience. Try to be subtle.

## QUOTES

Quoting someone can add an interesting aspect to a news release...if the quote is relevant or character revealing. You can even safely quote yourself, providing you write it as though someone else were quoting you.

For example, you would not say, "I started making this product because I found nothing else that would clean glassware as easily as Clearview."

Instead you could say something like this:

Mary Jones, inventor and manufacturer of Clearview, was an average housewife and stay-at-home mother until she discovered the formula for the glass cleaning product in 1977. That discovery turned her into one of our area's most successful entrepreneurs.

"Becoming a business woman was the furthest thing from my mind," Jones says.

"I hit on the formula quite by accident, and since I had not found anything on the market that would clean glassware as effectively, I decided I would manufacture it myself."

Although Clearview is a combination of common household cleaning solutions, which products and what proportions are a closely guarded secret. Jones claims that she was lucky that she had not mixed the wrong things. "I didn't learn until later that there are certain household cleaning products that create a poisonous gas when mixed together," she says.

As you can see, even though Mary Jones is actually the person writing this, she writes it in such a way that it sounds as though she is being interviewed.

Quotes are helpful to a reporter, for even if he/she is prompted by the news release to contact the sender for a personal interview, the reporter already has some quotes on hand, which will be useful when sitting down to write the story.

## SUPPLEMENTARY MATERIAL

Including background and supplementary material can often enhance the value of your news release.

For instance, the news release from *Business Tokyo* in Chapter 6 is a good example. The facts and figures shown on the charts and graphs included with this news release gave added dimension to the points being made.

There is no doubt that the "Humor Exam," included with Dr. Robertshaw's news release (also shown in Chapter 6), and the "Tackiness I.Q. Test," included with the news release on *The Encyclopedia of Bad Taste* (shown in Chapter 8), made the news releases more interesting.

Supplementary material can deal with many things. It could be question and answer sheets, quizzes, or

"I.Q. tests," such as those mentioned in the above paragraphs. It might be a biography or background sheet on an author or a business owner. It could be product reviews. It could be a tip sheet to help readers feel better, feel more relaxed, look better, look younger, look more successful, save money, make more money...the list is endless.

Some words of caution, however: keep the length of any supplementary material reasonably short.

A radio talk show producer told me of one news release she received that included seven pages of facts and figures—far too much for a busy media person to wade through. Two to four pages of supplementary material is normally enough.

## PHOTOGRAPHS

Photographs are often sent as supplementary material. They are especially useful when sending news releases to a television station for the purpose of getting on a talk show. A person does not have to be beautiful or handsome to get on a show, but I've never seen anyone on a talk show that was so physically unattractive that they made me uncomfortable just looking at them. So, I assume that before inviting a person on a show, a producer likes to know that the person photographs reasonably well and that his or her appearance will not be distracting.

Photographs of the author are often sent with a news release on a book. Sometimes a picture of a new product will be sent with a news release from a business.

If what you are trying to publicize would be enhanced by a photograph, use 8 x 10 glossy black and white, *professional quality* prints. If the picture is to be reproduced in a newspaper or magazine, do not send a colored print. If color is absolutely essential to showing the true character of a person or product, first determine if the magazine or newspaper has color capability (many aren't set up for color). If so, you may wish to send a color transparency...but never a colored print.

Never send your only copy of a picture to any branch of the media, not even to your local newspaper, for your chances of getting it back are between slim and none.

When including a photograph with a news release, do not assume that because you have included all the information in your news release this information will go along with the picture. I can't count the times that my editor has shown me a picture and asked, "Do you have any idea who this is or where I got it?"

To avoid confusion in case the photograph gets separated from the news release, type the information relevant to the picture on a self-adhesive label and stick it to the back of the photo. Or print the information clearly on the back of the picture with a black felt-tip pen. Never, never, never use a ballpoint pen on a photograph! Ballpoint pens can damage the photo, and the ink smears.

If there are two or more persons in a picture, be sure you identify them, from left to right.

And by all means, include the name, address, and telephone number of the sender on the back of the photograph.

## COVER LETTERS

Cover letters (called "pitch" letters in the trade) are often used to clarify or enhance a news release. However, persons untrained in getting publicity often seem to be confused as to when a cover letter should be included and when it is unnecessary.

As a rule of thumb, a cover letter is not necessary if everything you want and need to say is included in the news release itself. However, many, many times the news release does not contain all the pertinent information in which the receiver would be interested. For instance, if you need to give directions or are inviting a member of the press to be your guest at an event, a cover letter is necessary for clarification.

Sometimes a news release will be composed for general use in a large publicity campaign promoting Joe Doe and his product or book. But it does not include such information as where Joe Doe was born and raised, or where he went to high school or college, or where he lives now. That information is not relevant for general use, but it is *very* relevant to the folks in Joe's hometown, the kids with whom he went to high school and college, and to his friends and neighbors in the city in which he now resides.

Or Joe may be a member of an organization of which there are branches around the country with many members who would make good potential customers. Along with the general news release, a cover letter would be included that pointed out Joe's long affiliation with the organization and would subtly include some reason why it was felt that this organization would be particularly interested in his product or book.

But if you have nothing to say in the letter except "Enclosed is my news release on XX product (or upcoming event)," do not bother sending a cover letter.

## ORDERING INFORMATION

If you are trying to promote a product, be sure you include in the body of your news release all the information that a potential reader will need to order your product, such as your name, address, telephone number, and the price. This is especially important for home-based or other small businesses which otherwise may be hard to locate.

Orders from readers not only put money into your pocket, but they help you to know that an article was written in response to your news release that generated business.

When ordering, customers will often state in which publication and in which issue they read about your product. This gives you the opportunity to write to the publication and request a tear sheet of the article in question, which can then be used in future promotions. (Tear sheets are discussed later in this chapter.)

If you are concerned about including ordering information for fear it will sound too commercial, the following are sentences which have been used in news releases without being edited out.

- This product can be ordered by calling (xxx) xxx-xxxx.

- This product can be ordered by writing to XXX Company, at (its address), for ($ amount) postage paid price.

- This product is available at the XX Local Store.

- For further information, contact (name a contact person or department) at the XX Company, (followed by the address and telephone number).

A news release for a book could also include the information in the body of the release in the following manner:

A new book, entitled *Ten Sure-Footed Steps to Success* ($19.95) has just been published by XX Publishing Company, at 310 Main Street, Bergtown, CA 90001.

Author May Day, a former contracts specialist, gives useful tips on how a person can avoid business pitfalls and climb the ladder of success.

Granted, ordering information is sometimes edited out of a news release, but include it nevertheless and let it be the editor's decision whether it stays or is cut.

## FREE GIFTS

Though editors may sometimes cut ordering information from a news release, they never cut out the information on how a reader may obtain a free gift.

The free gift may be something like the Fun Mail Directory offered by Java Publishing Company (discussed in the previous chapter). The publisher reports that the company was still getting requests three years after the articles appeared in newspapers.

Java Publishing Company also had great success with another free gift it offered—a Foreclosure Facts information report. The report gave advice to people who were in danger of losing their homes and included an order form for a larger book Java had published on the subject.

The free gift may be some very inexpensive product connected with your business, or it could be a list of tips on anything that would be of interest to the readers of a particular publication.

For instance, a dress shop could offer a sheet on "Ten Ways A Working Woman Can Dress For Less." A kitchenware shop could offer a sheet on "Tips To Cut Your Food Budget." Both of these offers would probably get a healthy response from readers of the women's section of a newspaper, and they would certainly give the businesses recognition.

People love to get something for nothing, and editors know this. If your business receives publicity as a side benefit of your free offer, it just can't be helped, can it?

One word of caution: To make offering a free gift economically feasible, be sure you make it plain that the offer is good only if those interested send you a self-addressed stamped envelope (and state the size of the envelope that will be required and how much postage will be necessary).

You don't have to offer something in the mail if you're only interested in attracting customers locally. In this case you could offer a free sample to everyone who visits the store on some special designated day. This way new customers who come to your store learn where it is located and what you have to offer.

## NEWS SERVICES

If yours is a small, local business, and your potential customers will be found within a twenty to thirty mile radius of your establishment, then publicity in your local newspaper is probably all that you desire.

But if you have a product that could be used nationwide and do not have the time or patience to dig out the names of all the editors and publications you would like to reach, you may wish to hire a news service. (See the appendix for directories listing news services.)

These services will take your news release (or even the general information you provide on your business, product, or service) and write a news article in journalistic style, akin to what a reporter would write. If your news release is well written, very few if any changes would be made or even be necessary.

The article is typeset in newspaper format and is ready to be copied as is. The article is then included in a multi-page brochure of articles and sent to thousands (about 10,000) of publications.

When a publication receives this brochure, any article that is of interest can be clipped out and pasted up by its layout people, ready to be printed.

The advantages are that (1) the news services

reach thousands of markets that you might not have the time nor information to reach, (2) even if you have the time, the postage to mail 10,000 individual news releases would cost about $1,500-2,000 (depending on how you mailed them), and you would still have to worry about obtaining mailing lists, and (3) the service is a boon to anyone who is totally unable to write an effective news release.

The disadvantage is that these news services are expensive and a large percentage of the recipients of the brochure will not use your article. But if you want to reach a huge number of media people, the expense may be worth it in the long run.

## USING TEAR SHEETS FOR ADDITIONAL PUBLICITY

Throughout this book, you have seen examples of news releases and the resulting articles. Copies of such articles are referred to as "tear sheets," and have great value in obtaining additional publicity once you have been mentioned in print.

Getting publicity is a little bit like the old problem of: You can't get a job without experience, but you can't get experience without a job.

Getting that first article about you, your product, or service may be the most difficult step, for hat one publication prints about you often influences what others print about you. For example, one book reviewer, who preferred to remain anonymous, said, "Let's face it! There is a lot of copycat' in this business. If we see a good review from another publication, it makes us feel it's worth our time."

And you may recall that (in Chapter 5) TV producer/host Laura Buxton cited "...backup material, such as a newspaper article on a person, which indicated he or she would make a good guest" as one of the things she likes to see before inviting someone to be on her show.

In Chapter 8, Eldonna P. Lay and Associates mentioned previous articles on the book, *Green Five,* in its second stage news release. Tear sheets of these articles were sent along with the news release to add more "authority."

Therefore, without belaboring the point, make sure you keep a file of all the articles written about you, your product, or service. Then, when appropriate, send copies of these articles along with your subsequent news releases to aid in generating additional publicity.

Tear sheets can also be very valuable in sales promotions. For example, short articles are sometimes reprinted in sales brochures. However, if you decide to use an entire article in this manner, be aware that you should obtain written permission to reprint it from the publication in which it appeared or you may be open for a suit for copyright violation. On the other hand, excerpts and quotes from an article can be used in your sales material without having to get written permission.

Since people tend to believe the written word, a newspaper or magazine article supporting your product or service can be a real sales aid. One local mattress company had an article written about its mattresses blown up to poster size. The posters were then placed in the mattress departments of a chain of retail furniture stores which sold these mattresses. People stopped to read the giant newspaper article, then wanted to take a close look at the mattresses.

Gathering and using tear sheets sounds simple enough, doesn't it? Well, it's not. For one thing, unless you hire a national clipping service, which is quite expensive, it is sometimes difficult to obtain tear sheets.

Of course, if you are sending only one news release to one local newspaper, then you can check the newspaper and clip the article when it's published.

In most cases, however, you will be sending your news release to several publications at the same time. If all of these publications are local, you will need to keep track of all of them to see when an article is published. *Never* ask a *local* reporter or editor to send you a copy of the published article! It's highly insulting to reporters that you can't be bothered to read the publication even when you think it will contain a piece about you. Not only is such a request totally insensitive, but it can sometimes annoy press people so much that they will not even want to publish an article about you.

Look at it from their point of view. Reporters (and most editors) don't have secretaries to do their clerical work for them. These people work at top speed all the time just to meet their deadlines. Therefore, even if they are willing to do this for you, they don't have time.

One way to get around this problem is to explain that you may be out of town and you don't want to miss the article in case it is published while you are away. Therefore, you are giving the reporter or editor a self-addressed stamped postcard with one line on the back that says, "The article on _____(you)_____ will appear in the _____ edition." Tell the reporter or editor to just fill in the date and pop it in the mail so you will be able to buy a number of copies upon your return to the city. Publications usually have back copies for sale.

Sometimes it works; sometimes it doesn't. At least it is a reasonable request requiring a minimum of the editor's time and effort. As explained in Chapter 4, an editor or reporter often does not know exactly when an article will appear. But at least providing a postcard and offering to buy copies upon your return will not make it look as if you were too cheap and too lazy to buy and read the publication.

However, don't count on receiving the card. The pace at which journalists work often precludes remembering a postcard they stuck in a pending file on an article that has already gone to the layout people. Even if they do remember, they might have to check with the layout people to ascertain in which issue it will run. All of this is very time consuming and can make it hard to meet deadlines. If reporters don't meet their deadlines, they get fired. How many favors would you be willing to do for someone if it meant losing your very livelihood?

On the national level, editors understand why you would request tear sheets if their publications are not available in your area. For example, if you live in Ohio and send a news release to a newspaper in California, it would be hard for you to learn if it generated an article unless the editor lets you know. Therefore, in the cover letter that accompanies your news release, you can request that a tear sheet be sent without fear of offending the editor. Although you may not get a response, at least you won't offend anyone.

Sometimes a self-addressed postcard as described above works better on a national level. An editor occasionally makes the extra effort in that case.

Once you know in which issue an article will appear (or has appeared), it is not difficult to call the publication and find out how to order two or more copies. (You will always want at least two originals. Trust me! You may be using copies of these articles for years as backup for your subsequent news releases or for sales promotions. Not only do copies suffer from wear and tear after a time, but they may be accidentally misplaced.)

More often than not, if a publication prints something from your news release they will not notify you and you may never even know about it. This is especially true when sending out hundreds or thousands of releases to various publications. Probably the most common way of learning that an article has been published is through the responses you get from readers who want to order your product or wish further information on your service. Many times they will mention the specific issue in which they read about your product or service. Once you have that information, you can order copies of that issue. Frequently the interested reader will actually send a copy of the article as a reference to where they found out about you.

Getting tear sheers can be difficult but well worth your time and effort. So, persevere, and, by collecting copies of tear sheets, you will gain a valuable asset for publicity.

# CHAPTER 12

# PRACTICE EXERCISES

Reading about techniques for writing news releases is one thing, but actually writing them will help improve your skills tremendously. This chapter is designed to help you get the practice you need in order to gain competence and confidence as you master the art of writing news releases.

Strangely enough, we often learn best by bad examples. Therefore, before you attempt your practice releases, see if you can analyze what is wrong in the following examples.

## EXERCISE 1

Look at Exercise 1 on page 156. Analyze this release and find out what is wrong with it.

### Discussion

Does this news release contain complete information? Run it through the Five W's quiz.

**WHO**: LAP (Lose A Pound), a non-profit support organization for people who want to lose weight

**WHAT**: Is holding an open house
**WHEN**: 9 a.m. to 11 a.m., Sat., June 15
**WHERE**: First Community Church, 5th and Broadway, Bergtown
**WHY**: To celebrate its 25th anniversary

Is the name and telephone number for a contact person listed? Yes, but not until you reach the last line.

Would you be able to tell at a glance what this is about? No, for there is no informational, attention-grabbing headline.

Misspellings within the body of the release mark it as the work of a careless person.

Also, without a letterhead or the name of the organization listed at the top, there is nothing distinctive about this release.

Now let's examine the content, paragraph by paragraph.

1) Most of the essential information is listed, but the time the event takes place should be included here.

2) This explains the organization, but could be phrased more concisely.

3) What does the information in this paragraph have to do with the open house? Is the queen

---

## EXERCISE 1

LAP (Lose A Pound) is celebrating its 25th anniversary with an open house on  Sat., June 15, at the First Community Church, 5th and Broadway, Bergtown.

LAP is a non-profit organization that meets weekly as a support group to help members lose excess weight and reach their desired goals.  The club helps each member reach personal goals with weekly and monthly fun contests and lots of encouragement.  Dues are $4 a month.

LAP's queen for this year was Karen Martin, who reached her goal of losing 17 lbs., and graduated to STAT (Stay Thin and Trim).

New officers were elected in May.

One long-time members says, "I look forward each week to our meeting."

Open house will be 9 a.m. to 11 a.m., Sat., June 15, at the First Community Church, 5th and Broadway, Bergtown.  Anyway interested in additional information can contact May Borg at 555-0299.

---

being honored that day?  If so, that should be stated.

4)  This, too, is off the subject, unless the new officers will be presiding for the first time at the open house.  If that is the case, it should be made clear.  Also, if it is pertinent that new officers were elected, their names should be given.

5) Not only is this an inane quote, adding nothing to the news value of the story, but without the name of the person giving the quote, who cares?

6)  This is just a repeat of information already included in paragraph 1.

Now look on page 157 for a improved version of this release.

### LAP (Lose A Pound)
### An Organization For Losers

FOR IMMEDIATE RELEASE                    CONTACT:  May Borg
                                         TELEPHONE:  555-0299
May 28, 2005


LAP CELEBRATES 25 YEARS OF BEING A BUNCH OF LOSERS


LAP (Lose A Pound), a non-profit support group for people who wish to lose weight, is celebrating its 25th anniversary at an open house to be held from 9 to 11 a.m., Saturday, June 15, at the First Community Church, Fifth and Broadway, Bergtown.  The public is invited at no charge.

LAP meets weekly, and, through mutual encouragement and monthly contests, helps members lose excess pounds and reach their desired goals.  Karen Martin, who lost 17 pounds to reach her ideal weight, was named LAP's queen for this year and will be guest of honor at the open house.

LAP welcomes new members.  Dues are $4 per month.

Contact May Borg at 555-0299 for additional information about LAP and/or its open house.

### ###

*Revised news release for exercise 1.*

## EXERCISE 2

This time take a separate sheet of paper and analyze the release on the next page. Don't peek at the corrected copy on page 160 until after you have listed everything you can find that should be changed.

Do the exercise now before reading the discussion below.

### Discussion

Didn't you find it strange that an organization interested in the environment is having a meeting on the availability of health care? Yet, if the news release had been written to emphasize MIRE's concern over how the environment is affecting the health of the community (progress and disaster), then it makes sense and also adds the news value of proximity.

Now to examine the body of the release by paragraph.

1) This is not only a dull lead paragraph, but it does not give complete information as to where and when the meeting is to be held.

2) We might suspect that the "discussion" will confirm that no one is satisfied with the health care system, so there is nothing newsworthy here and it becomes an inane quote.

3) This sounds as if the public is invited to air its complaints, but who will ask and who will reply in the question-and-answer session following? Will there be a knowledgeable person with expertise in environmental health problems available?

4) This information should be included with the announcement of the meeting.

5) Anyone interested *may* join. Whether anyone *can*, I suppose depends on his own health.

## EXERCISE 2

MEN INTERESTED IN RESPONSIBLE ENVIRONMENT

August 16, 2005                        Contact: Stu Green 555-6051
                                                President
                                       Duke Astin 555-0392
                                                Publicity

FOR RELEASE AFTER SEPTEMBER 1

MEN INTERESTED IN RESPONSIBLE ENVIRONMENT
TO STUDY HEALTH CARE AVAILABILITY

Health care availability will be studied by Men Interested in Responsible Environment (MIRE) at its meeting on Sept. 13.

"We will discuss whether or not we are satisfied with our health care system," says Stu Green, president of MIRE. "We will explore questions such as: How is the environment affecting our health? Does everyone have access to health care in our community? Is the cost too high?"

Members of the public are invited to come and share their views on what they think of health care and to discuss any problems they have had in this area. A question and answer session will follow.

The meeting will be held at the Green residence, 457 Poe Street, at 10 a.m.

Anyone interested can join MIRE at any meeting.

## MEN INTERESTED IN RESPONSIBLE ENVIRONMENT
### 457 Poe Street
### Bergtown, CA 90001

```
CONTACT: Stu Green, President          August 16, 2005
         555-6051
     OR: Duke Astin, Publicity
         555-0392
                                       FOR RELEASE ON: Sept. 6


         THE ENVIRONMENT'S EFFECT ON COMMUNITY HEALTH:
            A SERIOUS PROBLEM OR SIMPLE HYSTERIA?
```

Hazardous waste, acid rain, and polluted air have all been cited as causes of common ailments in today's society.  But how is the environment affecting the health of Bergtown's citizens?

Men Interested in Responsible Environment (MIRE) will discuss that question at its next meeting, to be held at 10 a.m., Friday, September 13, at the home of President Stu Green, 457 Poe Street.

"We will also explore whether adequate health care is available for those who have suffered because of environmental pollutants, and what city government is doing to offset the costs," says Green.

Green, an expert on environmental health hazards, will lead the group discussion and the question-and-answer period following.

The public is invited to come share its views and experiences in this area.  There is no charge.

### ###

*Revised news release for Exercise 2.*

## EXERCISE 3

Contact Martha Steel 555-6741
Release by July 19/July 26


SENIORS PLAN UNIQUE SALE


Crafters of all types will be attracted to a craft supply sale at
the Bergtown Senior Center on Friday, July 19, 11 a.m. to 4 p.m.
There will be supplies for both hobby crafters and professionals.
Dollmakers, quilters, artists, needleworkers, dressmakers, jewel-
ers and weavers will be attracted to this sale.  Fabric, yarn,
ribbon, lace, books, latch hook, notions and much more will be
offered at reasonable prices.  Crafters will have an opportunity
to receive and share ideas.

The following week on Friday, July 26, there will be an Attic
Treasures Sale from 11 a.m. to 4 p.m.  Donations from Center members and friends will be sold at reasonable prices.  Items range
from garage sale stuff to curios and antiques.  At the same time,
you can share a plant with someone you love (or even a stranger)
during the exchange and sale.

Donations for these special events will be gladly accepted up to
the day of the sales.

## EXERCISE 3

Make all necessary corrections for Exercise 3 above. See if you can determine which news values are involved in this release.  And don't forget to look for complete information. Turn the page for a revised version and explanation.

**BERGTOWN SENIOR CENTER**
**2591 Oakwood Avenue**
**Bergtown, CA 90001**


July 4, 2005                              CONTACT:  Martha Steel

FOR IMMEDIATE RELEASE                     TELEPHONE:  555-6741


LOW PRICES ON ARTS AND CRAFTS SUPPLIES EXPECTED TO DRAW MANY
HOBBYISTS AND PROFESSIONALS TO SENIOR CENTER SALE

Who doesn't love a bargain?  Artisans and craftsmen—whether hobbyists or professionals—will find attractive buys on everything from
fabric, yarn, ribbon and lace to books, latch hooks, notions, and
more at the Senior Center sale.

The event will be held at the Senior Center, 2591 Oakwood Ave.,
from 11 a.m. to 4 p.m., Friday, July 19.  Arts and crafts enthusiasts will have an opportunity to stock up on supplies at below
market prices and exchange ideas on their areas of interest.

On Friday, July 26, there will be an Attic Treasures sale from 11
a.m. to 4 p.m., at the same location.  Merchandise will range from
curios and antiques to items usually found at garage sales—all at
reasonable prices.  Donations will be welcomed at the Senior
Center until July 18.

As an added attraction, those attending are encouraged to bring
plants which they would like to trade.


###

*Revised news release for Exercise 3.*

## Discussion

Let's look at the original release on page 161. If the news is not released until July 19, the day of the sale, or even worse, until July 26, the day of the second part of the sale, the Senior Center will have wasted its postage, for the public will not have gotten word in time to attend.

On the other points, let's take them one by one.

1) Does the headline excite you? Does it even tell you what kind of sale is being held? And how "unique" is selling fabric, yarn, and ribbon, etc.?

2) Despite the fact that there are no such words as "crafters," "dollmakers," and "needleworkers" in the dictionary, we know what these words mean. Although we are told twice that these "crafters" will be attracted to the sale (which is, at best, a hopeful assumption), the address of the Senior Center is not given. In order to run an item on the event, an editor would have to either call the contact person or look up the Senior Center in the telephone directory. If the editor is running short on time and has plenty of other items competing for the space, the lack of an address could be the deciding factor for tossing this news release into the wastebasket.

3) The use of "at reasonable prices" is redundant. Another phrase, such as "at bargain rates," should be used. Also, "stuff" brings visions of "junk." What plants have to do with an Attic Treasures sale, I am not sure.

4) Although we are told donations will be gladly accepted, no indication is given as to where the donations should be delivered.

Thousands of news releases such as this are received by newspapers across the country every year, and most don't make it into print because of the various errors and/or lack of complete information.

To keep this news release from being among the eighty percent which get trashed, the version on page 162 would be preferable.

## EXERCISE 4

Now that you have had an opportunity to critique a few news releases, it's time to try out your newly acquired skills and write some of your own.

In this example, a scenario will be outlined, and from the information given, you are to compose a news release. Try to include as many news values as possible.

Homer Bryce has developed a formula for a solution that will clean carbon deposits off pots and pans with little effort and without damaging the surface. He calls it KLEAN KWIC.

Homer has a master's degree in chemistry and worked for a firm called Industrial Chemical Enterprises (ICE) for thirty-one years before taking early retirement last year. During his career, he rose to the rank of second vice-president in charge of research.

Homer, now 56, has perfected his cleaner and is manufacturing it in his garage. A few retail stores in his area are carrying the product, but for the most part, it is unknown at this time.

He wants to get the word to the public on a national level and intends, with the help of his wife, Carol, to sell the product by mail. He has a free brochure that he will send to anyone who requests it, and sends a self-addressed stamped envelope.

Very enthusiastic about his discovery, Homer has many good things to say about his product. (You get to make up a quote.)

He hopes to develop additional cleaners in the future, so he has named his company Helpful Household Products, Inc. The mailing address on his business letterhead is P.O. Box 100, Bergtown, CA 90001. His telephone number is (714) 555-2345.

Before you start writing, ask yourself a few questions.

**1) Who will benefit most from using this product?**

The answer, obviously, is people who clean pots and pans. Since it is usually the woman of the house who gets this dubious honor, this is the person to whom you will address the news release.

**2) What sections of a newspaper or which national magazines is the homemaker most likely to read?**

Today's women, often involved in careers as well as being homemakers, cannot be as easily categorized as their mothers. But many still enjoy the traditional aspects of their dual roles, and quite likely would read the food and lifestyle sections of a newspaper, as well as one or more "women's" magazines.

**3) In addition to homemakers, who else would care about this story?**

Since Homer is 56, how he started a business after retiring would be a good story for a "seniors" column or a magazine slanted toward seniors. Yet, he would still have the opportunity to mention his product. After all, seniors also clean pots and pans. It would also be a good story for a newspaper's business section or a magazine slanted toward business opportunities.

Because of the wide number of possible markets, rather than writing just one news release, write one for each of the markets we have identified: homemakers, seniors, and businesses.

**Discussion**

In choosing your headlines, slant each one to its specific market. For example, on the release aimed at homemakers, your headline might read:

NEW CLEANING PRODUCT GETS
CINDERELLA-HOMEMAKERS OUT OF THE
KITCHEN IN TIME FOR THE BALL

Then your first paragraph might read:

With no fairy godmother and her magic wand to come to the rescue, a homemaker can sometimes feel like poor Cinderella, scrubbing mountains of pots and pans. But KLEAN KWIC, a revolutionary new product discovered by veteran chemist Homer Bryce, has changed all that.

If your news release is slanted toward seniors, your headline might read like this:

RETIREMENT OPENS THE DOOR
TO NEW OPPORTUNITIES

Your first paragraph could address Homer's expertise, which he has put to new use. You might write something like this:

After 31 years with Industrial Chemical Enterprises (ICE), Homer Bryce, 56, thought his days of doing research were over when he retired last year. He planned to play golf and do some traveling. But when his wife, Carol, complained about baked-on grease and grime making it nearly impossible to clean pots and pans and restore them to their original condition, Bryce could not resist the challenge.

In a news release aimed at a business opportunities magazine or a newspaper's business section, slant your headline accordingly. It might read like this:

VETERAN CHEMIST DISCOVERS
NEW BUSINESS OPPORTUNITIES ALONG
WITH REVOLUTIONARY NEW CLEANING
PRODUCT

The first paragraph would emphasize the business aspects and might read like this:

"I never expected to be in business for myself," says Homer Bryce, 56, who retired last year as second vice-president in charge of research for Industrial Chemical Enterprises (ICE). "But opportunity did not just knock, it hit me over the head."

All right, enough hand-holding. It's time for you to solo. Write a news release for each market. Then look at the check list below to see if you covered everything.

## Check List For Exercise 4

1) Did you write your news releases on Homer's business letterhead stationery?

2) Did you put FOR IMMEDIATE RELEASE near the top?

3) Did you show the name and telephone number of the contact person?

4) Did you have attention-grabbing headlines?

5) Did you emphasize an appropriate news value in each release?

6) When quoting Homer, did the quotes show his character or provide significant information?

7) Did you indicate that a free brochure was available and give an address?

8) Did you check your spelling to make sure your news releases looked professional?

9) If you were the editor receiving your news releases, would they interest you?

If you can answer "Yes" to the above questions, you are doing fine.

## EXERCISE 5

Next, using our old standby, the Bergtown Gardening Club, determine what is wrong with the following news release, then rewrite it.

## Discussion

Gag reflex time! Right?

This is an example of how "empty" adjectives can ruin a news release. Untrained publicity chairpersons often write flowery news releases in an effort to make an event sound more exciting. But editors are not favorably impressed.

What is the most significant news value in that release? Don't you think it would be that the governor's wife is expected to attend (eminence and prominence)? Yet that information was buried at the bottom.

The name and telephone number for a contact person were there, but they, too, were at the bottom and not where you would spot them at a glance.

And I am sure you noticed there was no headline.

Now rewrite the release emphasizing the most pertinent news values, and stick to the facts using adjectives only when they are really relevant. Keep in mind that an editor looks for clear, concise, readable copy.

## EXERCISE 5

## BERGTOWN GARDENING CLUB
### 233 Holly Hock Avenue
### Bergtown, CA 90001

The elegant Bergtown Gardening Club, composed of some of Bergtown's leading, most glamorous citizens, is holding its exciting installation luncheon at 12:30 p.m., Friday, May 15, at the posh Midtown restaurant, located at 1222 Ocean Blvd., Bergtown.

The forceful new president, the enchanting Mary Gold, will hoist her gavel to begin her second term in office on that auspicious occasion.

The governor's beautiful wife, a gardening enthusiast, is expected to attend.

For further information, call Lily White at 555-1001

### ###

## EXERCISE 6

In this exercise you are given the bare facts with which to write a COMMUNITY CALENDAR LISTING.

**WHO**:  Bergtown All-Faith Church, 444 Saint Helen Drive, Bergtown, CA 90001

**WHAT**:  Is holding a luncheon and fashion show. The clothes will be furnished by the Women's Choice Shoppe.  Tickets are $5 and the event is open to the public.

**WHEN**:  12 p.m., Saturday, May 30, 20—

**WHERE**:  The Bergtown All-Faith Church's recreation hall, 444 Saint Helen Dr., Bergtown.

**WHY**:  To raise money to aid famine victims in Somalia, Africa.

**CONTACTS**:  Mary Godley (555-5443) is publicity chairwoman.  Joanna Priest (555-9045) is in charge of reservations.

Write your release using only the information given above.  Then compare your release with the one on page 169.

## ADDITIONAL EXERCISES

For further practice, pick stories from your local newspaper, and using the facts given, see if you can write a news release that might have generated each story.

You may find that, initially, you are slow in dreaming up attention-grabbing headlines or that you neglect to include a piece of vital information.  But practice makes perfect, so do not let those little things discourage you while you are learning.  You'll be amazed at how soon you will become adept at writing news releases if you continue to practice.

So, good luck, and may you find the success you seek by learning to write effective news releases.

**BERGTOWN ALL-FAITH CHURCH**
**444 Saint Helen Drive**
**Bergtown, CA 90001**

COMMUNITY SERVICE ANNOUNCEMENT                    CONTACT:  Mary Godley
                                                 Telephone:  555-5443

Date:  May 1, 2005

BERGTOWN ALL-FAITH CHURCH SPONSORS LUNCHEON AND FASHION SHOW
TO AID FAMINE VICTIMS IN SOMALIA, AFRICA

Fashions from Women's Choice Shoppe will be displayed at a luncheon and fashion show to be held at 12 p.m., Saturday, May 30, in
the Bergtown All-Faith Church's recreation hall, 444 Saint Helen
Dr., Bergtown.

Tickets are $5 and the event is open to the public.  For reserva-
tions, call Joanna Priest at 555-9045.

For further information, contact Mary Godley at 555-5443.

### 

*Revised news release for Exercise 6.*

# APPENDIX

# REFERENCES

Most of the books listed on the following pages can be found in your local public library or bookstore. However, if they do not have them, you can write to the publishers for further information.

Books listed here will help you find information on the following: newspapers, TV and radio stations, magazine and trade publications, newsletters, news services, how to improve your writing and journalism skills, getting publicity and developing newsworthy ideas.

## DIRECTORIES

ALL-IN-ONE DIRECTORY
Gebbie Press
P.O. Box 1000
New Paltz, NY 12561
Annual listing of print and broadcast media.

BACON'S PUBLICITY CHECKER
14 East Jackson Blvd.
Chicago, IL 60604
Lists newspapers, news services, and syndicates.

BROADCASTING CABLE YEARBOOK
Broadcasting Publications, Inc.
1705 DeSales Street, N.W.
Washington, D.C. 20036
Directory of broadcast media.

EDITOR & PUBLISHER INTERNATIONAL
YEARBOOK
Editor and Publisher
11 West 19th Street
New York, NY 10011
Daily and weekly newspapers, syndicates, and news services in the United States, Canada, and other countries.

ENCYCLOPEDIA OF ASSOCIATIONS
Gale Research, Inc.
835 Penobscot Building
Detroit, MI 48226-4094
Lists private, commercial and governmental societies, associations, clubs, and other organizations.

FINDER BINDER
Gary Beals Advertising and Public Relations
4679 Vista Street
San Diego, CA 92116-4848
Lists newspaper, TV, and radio personnel.

GALE DIRECTORY OF PUBLICATIONS
AND BROADCAST MEDIA
Gale Research, Inc.
835 Penobscot Building
Detroit, MI 48226-4094
Three volumes with 36,000 entries.

HUDSON'S NEWSLETTER DIRECTORY
P.O. Box 311
Rhinebeck, NY 12572
Lists newsletters.

LITERARY MARKET PLACE
245 West 17th Street
New York, NY 10011
Lists news services, feature syndicates, radio and TV programs, newspapers, and magazines which feature books and/or book reviews.

MEDIA GUIDE INTERNATIONAL
Directories International
150 Fifth Avenue
New York, NY 10011
Business/professional publications.

NEWSLETTERS IN PRINT
Gale Research, Inc.
835 Penobscot Building
Detroit, MI 48226-4094
A descriptive guide to newsletters, bulletins, digests, updates, and similar serial publications.

OXBRIDGE DIRECTORY OF
NEWSLETTERS
Oxbridge Communications, Inc.
150 Fifth Avenue, Suite 636
New York, NY 10011
Directory of newsletters.

RADIO CONTACTS
Larimi Communications Assoc., Ltd.
5 West 37th Street
New York, NY 10018
An annual directory listing of local, network, and syndicated radio programs.

THE STANDARD PERIODICAL DIRECTORY
Oxbridge Communications, Inc.
150 Fifth Avenue, Suite 636
New York, NY 10011
Lists 75,000 periodicals in the United States and Canada.

STANDARD RATES AND DATA SERVICE
Standard Rates and Data Service, Inc.
3004 Glenview Road
Wilmette, IL 60091
Multi-volume series, one of which lists newspapers with information on readership and advertising rates.

SYNDICATED COLUMNIST DIRECTORY
Larimi Communications Assoc., Ltd.
5 West 37th Street
New York, NY 10018
Columnists for print and broadcast media.

TELEVISION CONTACTS
Larimi Communications Assoc., Ltd.
5 West 37th Street
New York, NY 10018
Annual directory listing of local, network, and syndicated TV programs.

TV NEWS
Larimi Communications Assoc., Ltd.
5 West 37th Street
New York, NY 10018
An annual that lists news programs on local and network TV stations.

ULRICH'S INTERNATIONAL PERIODICAL
DIRECTORY
R.R. Bowker Company
121 Chanlon Road
New Providence, NJ 07974
Probably the most complete periodical directory in print.

THE WORKING PRESS OF THE NATION
The National Research Bureau
225 W. Wacker Drive, Suite 2275
Chicago, IL 60606
Five volumes listing newspapers, magazines, TV and Radio stations complete with individual names of editors, disc jockeys, news directors, etc.

WRITER'S MARKET
Writer's Digest Books
1507 Dana Avenue
Cincinnati, OH 45207
Comprehensive list of trade, technical and professional journals and consumer magazines.

## RESOURCES ON PUBLICITY AND DEVELOPING NEWSWORTHY IDEAS

A WHACK ON THE SIDE OF THE HEAD
by Roger Von Oech
Warner Books
666 Fifth Avenue, 9th Floor
New York, NY 10103
An innovative book showing how to think creatively.

CHASE'S ANNUAL EVENTS
by William and Helen Chase
Contemporary Books, Inc.
180 North Michigan Avenue
Chicago, IL 60601
An annual publication listing specially designated days, weeks, and months.

THE COMPLETE GUIDE TO
SELF-PUBLISHING
by Tom and Marilyn Ross
Writer's Digest Books
1507 Dana Avenue
Cincinnati, OH 45207
Step-by-step guide to self-publishing and book publicity.

GETTING PUBLICITY
by Tana Fletcher and Julia Rockler
Self-Counsel Press
1481 Charlotte Road
North Vancouver, British Columbia V7J 1H1
Emphasizes low-cost, do-it-yourself promotional strategies. Many examples of news releases.

GETTING THE MESSAGE OUT
by Michael M. Klepper
Prentice-Hall Press
15 Columbus Circle, 15 floor
New York, NY 10023
How to get and use radio and television airtime.

HOMEMADE MONEY
by Barbara Brabec
Betterway Publications, Inc.
P.O. Box 219
Crozet, VA 22932
Written for people who operate home-based businesses. Contains many good examples of news releases.

HOW TO GET PUBLICITY
by William Parkhurst
Random House, Inc.
201 E. 50th Street, 31st Floor
New York, NY 10022
Explains how to get interviews. Covers the basics of writing news releases and designing press kits.

HOW TO GET PUBLICITY IN NEWSPAPERS
by Arnold Furst
Borden Publishing Company
2623 San Fernando Road
Los Angeles, CA 90065
Outlines techniques for getting newspaper coverage.

HOW TO KEEP YOUR PRESS RELEASE OUT OF THE WASTEBASKET
by Holland Cooke
Holland Cooke
3220 N. Street N.W.
Washington, D.C. 20007
The basics of writing news releases by a broadcast professional.

LESLY'S PUBLIC RELATIONS HANDBOOK
by Philip Lesly
Prentice-Hall, Inc.
15 Columbus Circle, 15th Flr.
New York, NY 10023
A huge resource dealing with all aspects of getting publicity and working with the media.

NEWS RELEASES AND BOOK PUBLICITY
by Dan Poynter
Para Publishing
P.O. Box 4232
Santa Barbara, CA 93140
This 45 page report deals specifically with book publicity.

ON THE AIR
by Al Parinello
The Career Press Inc.
180 5th Avenue
Hawthorne, NJ 07507
Tells how to get on radio and TV talk shows and what to do when you get there.

PUBLICITY FOR BOOKS AND AUTHORS
by Peggy Glenn
Aames-Allen Publishing Company
1106 Main Street
Huntington Beach, CA 92648-2719
Creative publicity ideas for authors and publishers.

PUBLICITY FOR VOLUNTEERS
by Virginia Bortin
Walker & Company
720 Fifth Avenue
New York, NY 10019
A publicity handbook for churches and non-profit organizations.

PUBLICITY HANDBOOK FOR CHURCHES AND CHRISTIAN ORGANIZATIONS
by Jim A. Vitti
Zondervan Publishing Corp.
1415 Lake Drive SE
Grand Rapids, MI 49506
Publicity source book for religious organizations.

PUBLICITY KIT
by Jeannette Smith
John Wiley & Sons, Inc.
605 Third Avenue
New York, NY 10158
A guide for entrepreneurs, small businesses, and non-profit organizations.

THE PUBLICITY MANUAL
by Kate Kelly
Visibility Enterprises
11 Rockwood Drive
Larchmont, NY 10538
How to get publicity and develop good relations.

RADIO TALK SHOW SYSTEM
Pacesetter Publications
P.O. Box 24174
Denver, CO 80224
This manual explains how to get on radio talk shows, how to prepare for the interview, and how to create an effective press kit.

TV PR
by Wicke Chambers and Spring Asher
Chase Communications, Inc.
1776 Nancy Creek Bluff NW
Atlanta, GA 30327
How to promote yourself, your product, your service, or your organization on television.

THE WRITER'S GUIDE TO SELF-PROMOTION AND PUBLICITY
by Elane Feldman
Writer's Digest Books
1507 Dana Avenue
Cincinnati, OH 45207
How authors can publicize and promote their own books.

## RESOURCES FOR DEVELOPING WRITING AND JOURNALISM SKILLS

BASIC NEWS WRITING
by Melvin Mencher
William C. Brown Publishers
25 Kessel Ct., Ste. 201
Madison, WI 53711
Covers the basic elements of news writing.

COPYWRITER'S HANDBOOK
by Nat Bodian
ISI Press
3501 Market Street
Philadelphia, PA 19104
Covers advertising and promotion copywriting and headline writing techniques.

EDITORIAL AND PERSUASIVE WRITING
by Harry W. Stonecipher
Communication Arts Books
141 Halstead Ave
Mamaroneck, NY 10543
Discusses every aspect of print and electronic editorial writing.

THE EVERYDAY ENGLISH HANDBOOK
by Leonard J. Rosen
Doubleday & Company
666 5th Avenue
New York, NY 10103
A concise summary of English grammar, contemporary usage, punctuation, and capitalization.

FUNDAMENTALS OF JOURNALISM
by Spencer Crump
McGraw-Hill, Inc.
1221 Avenue of the Americas
New York, NY 10020
An introduction to journalistic writing.


GETTING THE WORDS RIGHT
by Theodore A. Rees Cheney
Writer's Digest Books
1507 Dana Avenue
Cincinnati, OH 45207
Teaches how to revise, edit, and rewrite. Includes many helpful examples.


MAKE EVERY WORD COUNT
by Gary Provost
Writer's Digest Books
1507 Dana Avenue
Cincinnati, OH 45207
A basic guide for learning good writing techniques.


NEWSWRITING FOR THE ELECTRONIC MEDIA
by Daniel E. Garvey and William L. Rivers
Wodsdworth Publishing Company
Belmont, CA 94002
Principles and applications of newswriting. Includes many examples.


NEWS HEADLINES
by Harold Evans
Holt, Rinehart and Winston
6277 Sea Harbor Dr.
Orlando, FL 32887
How to write captivating headlines.


PERSUASIVE WRITING
by Herman Holtz
McGraw-Hill Book Inc.
1221 Avenue of the Americas
New York, NY 10020
Persuasive writing techniques used in advertising and publicity. Includes news releases.


WRITE RIGHT!
by Jan Venolia
Ten Speed Press
P.O. Box 7123
Berkeley, CA 94707
Covers proper word usage, punctuation, grammar, and style.


THE WRITER'S WORKBOOK
by Judith Appelbaum and Florence Janovic
The Pushcart Press
P.O. Box 380
Wainscott, NY 11975
A manual for improving writing skills.


WRITING ON BOTH SIDES OF THE BRAIN
by Henriette Anne Klauser
Writer's Digest Books
1507 Dana Avenue
Cincinnati, OH 45207
Creative writing techniques.


WRITING WITH PRECISION
by Jefferson D. Bates
Acropolis Books Ltd.
2400 17th Street, NW
Washington, DC 20009
Techniques on improving writing style and becoming a better writer.

# INDEX